**INTRODUCING
ISSUES WITH
OPPOSING
VIEWPOINTS**®

# Genetic
# Engineering

Lauri S. Friedman, *Book Editor*

**GREENHAVEN PRESS**
*A part of Gale, Cengage Learning*

**GALE**
**CENGAGE Learning·**

Detroit • New York • San Francisco • New Haven, Conn • Waterville, Maine • London

GALE
CENGAGE Learning·

Elizabeth Des Chenes, *Managing Editor*

© 2012 Greenhaven Press, a part of Gale, Cengage Learning

Gale and Greenhaven Press are registered trademarks used herein under license.

*For more information, contact:*
Greenhaven Press
27500 Drake Rd.
Farmington Hills, MI 48331-3535
Or you can visit our Internet site at gale.cengage.com

For product information and technology assistance, contact us at

Gale Customer Support, 1-800-877-4253
For permission to use material from this text or product, submit all requests online at www.cengage.com/permissions

Further permissions questions can be e-mailed to permissionrequest@cengage.com

Articles in Greenhaven Press anthologies are often edited for length to meet page requirements. In addition, original titles of these works are changed to clearly present the main thesis and to explicitly indicate the author's opinion. Every effort is made to ensure that Greenhaven Press accurately reflects the original intent of the authors. Every effort has been made to trace the owners of copyrighted material.

Cover image © emin kuliyev/Shutterstock.com

| LIBRARY OF CONGRESS CATALOGING-IN-PUBLICATION DATA |
| --- |
| Genetic engineering / Lauri S. Friedman, editor. |

Genetic engineering / Lauri S. Friedman, editor.
  p. cm. -- (Introducing issues with opposing viewpoints)
  Summary: "Genetic Engineering: Is Genetic Engineering Ethical?; Should Society Embrace Genetically Engineered Food?; How Should Genetic Engineering Be Regulated?"-- Provided by publisher.
  Includes bibliographical references and index.
  ISBN 978-0-7377-5680-7 (hardback)
  1. Genetic engineering--Juvenile literature. 2. Genetic engineering--Moral and ethical aspects--Juvenile literature. I. Friedman, Lauri S.
  QH442.G44317 2012
  174.2--dc23
                                                          2011028274

Printed in the United States of America
1 2 3 4 5 6 7 15 14 13 12 11

# Contents

## Chapter 3: How Should Genetic Engineering Be Regulated?

# Foreword

Indulging in a wide spectrum of ideas, beliefs, and perspectives is a critical cornerstone of democracy. After all, it is often debates over differences of opinion, such as whether to legalize abortion, how to treat prisoners, or when to enact the death penalty, that shape our society and drive it forward. Such diversity of thought is frequently regarded as the hallmark of a healthy and civilized culture. As the Reverend Clifford Schutjer of the First Congregational Church in Mansfield, Ohio, declared in a 2001 sermon, "Surrounding oneself with only like-minded people, restricting what we listen to or read only to what we find agreeable is irresponsible. Refusing to entertain doubts once we make up our minds is a subtle but deadly form of arrogance." With this advice in mind, Introducing Issues with Opposing Viewpoints books aim to open readers' minds to the critically divergent views that comprise our world's most important debates.

Introducing Issues with Opposing Viewpoints simplifies for students the enormous and often overwhelming mass of material now available via print and electronic media. Collected in every volume is an array of opinions that captures the essence of a particular controversy or topic. Introducing Issues with Opposing Viewpoints books embody the spirit of nineteenth-century journalist Charles A. Dana's axiom: "Fight for your opinions, but do not believe that they contain the whole truth, or the only truth." Absorbing such contrasting opinions teaches students to analyze the strength of an argument and compare it to its opposition. From this process readers can inform and strengthen their own opinions, or be exposed to new information that will change their minds. Introducing Issues with Opposing Viewpoints is a mosaic of different voices. The authors are statesmen, pundits, academics, journalists, corporations, and ordinary people who have felt compelled to share their experiences and ideas in a public forum. Their words have been collected from newspapers, journals, books, speeches, interviews, and the Internet, the fastest growing body of opinionated material in the world.

Introducing Issues with Opposing Viewpoints shares many of the well-known features of its critically acclaimed parent series, Opposing Viewpoints. The articles are presented in a pro/con format, allowing readers to absorb divergent perspectives side by side. Active reading questions preface each viewpoint, requiring the student to approach the material thoughtfully and carefully. Useful charts, graphs, and cartoons supplement each article. A thorough introduction provides readers with crucial background on an issue. An annotated bibliography points the reader toward articles, books, and websites that contain additional information on the topic. An appendix of organizations to contact contains a wide variety of charities, nonprofit organizations, political groups, and private enterprises that each hold a position on the issue at hand. Finally, a comprehensive index allows readers to locate content quickly and efficiently.

Introducing Issues with Opposing Viewpoints is also significantly different from Opposing Viewpoints. As the series title implies, its presentation will help introduce students to the concept of opposing viewpoints and learn to use this material to aid in critical writing and debate. The series' four-color, accessible format makes the books attractive and inviting to readers of all levels. In addition, each viewpoint has been carefully edited to maximize a reader's understanding of the content. Short but thorough viewpoints capture the essence of an argument. A substantial, thought-provoking essay question placed at the end of each viewpoint asks the student to further investigate the issues raised in the viewpoint, compare and contrast two authors' arguments, or consider how one might go about forming an opinion on the topic at hand. Each viewpoint contains sidebars that include at-a-glance information and handy statistics. A Facts About section located in the back of the book further supplies students with relevant facts and figures.

Following in the tradition of the Opposing Viewpoints series, Greenhaven Press continues to provide readers with invaluable exposure to the controversial issues that shape our world. As John Stuart Mill once wrote: "The only way in which a human being can make some approach to knowing the whole of a subject is by hearing what can be said about it by persons of every variety of opinion and studying all modes in which it can be looked at by every character of mind. No wise man ever acquired his wisdom in any mode but this." It is to this principle that Introducing Issues with Opposing Viewpoints books are dedicated.

# Introduction

Any discussion about genetic engineering is simultaneously a discussion about eugenics, which is the process of affecting, for good or bad, the genetic makeup of society. Eugenics can be neutral, natural, or positive (such as when smart, talented, healthy people reproduce to make more smart, talented, healthy people) or negative (such as when people with undesirable traits are persecuted, sterilized, or even killed so as to limit their numbers). At its heart, eugenics is a form of selective breeding, and whether genetic engineering will encourage an evil version of it is passionately debated.

Opponents of genetic engineering are wary of its applications that aim to eradicate diseases, handicaps, or even physical traits that might be judged by some as undesirable (such as big noses or broad foreheads). Opponents argue that although being born with a disorder such as Down syndrome or autism makes life more challenging, such traits deserve to remain in the gene pool. The vast variety of people, even sick or challenged ones, are part of God's mysterious plan, say some; others think that all human beings are at risk once society begins selectively deciding who should get a chance at life. Columnist Chuck Colson is one person who fears this. He opposes genetic engineering techniques that could allow geneticists to screen for, and ultimately discard, embryos that have a high risk of being born with the cognitive and communicative disorder known as autism. "They are not 'curing' autism or even making life better for autistic people," he argues. "Their plan is to eliminate autism by eliminating autistic people."[1]

Likewise, Colson and others oppose genetic tests that make it possible to identify a fetus's risk of Down syndrome before he or she is born. As a result of such technology, fewer Down syndrome children are born in contemporary America than in the past, because many parents who learn of the risk in the second trimester of pregnancy decide to abort the child at that time. In fact, researchers at Children's Hospital in Boston found that between 1989 and 2005, prenatal genetic testing led to a 15 percent decrease in births of babies with Down syndrome in the United States. Researchers concluded that if testing had not been available, they would have expected to see a 34 percent *increase* in Down syndrome births during this period, given the later age at which the sampled women had chosen to have children (since older mothers have a greater risk of having a child with Down syndrome).

In other words, prenatal genetic testing directly led to the abortion of fetuses at risk for Down syndrome, and thus the practice is opposed by those who view genetic engineering as a biotechnological form of discrimination that will lead to the elimination of whole groups of people. Referring to people with Down syndrome as an "endangered population," Colson warns, "This utilitarian view of life inevitably leads us exactly where the Nazis were creating a master race. Can't we see it?"[2]

Yet proponents of genetic engineering do not believe it would encourage discrimination and genocide but rather the improvement of the human race as a whole. First, they point out that for centuries, even without the availability of genetic engineering technologies, humans have labeled other groups as inferior and tried to eradicate or exploit them. Slavery, the Holocaust, and other events of mass slaughter or exploitation are offered as proof that genetic engineering is not necessary for certain groups of humans to exploit other groups. "Let's face it, plenty of unenhanced humans have been quite capable of believing that millions of their fellow unenhanced humans were inferiors who needed to be eradicated," writes *Reason* science correspondent Ronald Bailey.[3] Conversely, Bailey thinks genetically engineered people would be less prone to such exploitation because they would develop superior institutions and abilities that would protect them from such harm. "As liberal political institutions have spread and strengthened, they have increasingly restrained technologically superior groups from automatically wiping out less advanced peoples (which was usual throughout most of history)," Bailey points out. "I suspect that this dynamic will continue in the future as biotechnology, nanotechnology, and computational technologies progressively increase people's capabilities and widen their choices."[4] In other words, Bailey thinks that genetic engineering will strengthen humans as a group, making them more equal and less prone to the kind of eugenic atrocities that have occurred in the past.

In addition, regarding genetic tests that have resulted in the decrease of Down syndrome births, supporters of genetic engineering argue that society has long used a variety of techniques, tools, and therapies to help people avoid giving birth to a diseased child. Beginning with centuries-old cultural taboos on incest—which typically produces children with crippling genetic abnormalities—to modern diagnostic blood tests that can determine whether a person is a genetic carrier of Tay-Sachs disease or cystic fibrosis before they are even pregnant—humans tend to accept, and wholeheartedly embrace, technologies that can help them produce the healthiest, smartest, most talented children possible.

Indeed, to seek a particular kind of child is natural and even routine, argues Harvard psychology professor Steven Pinker, who has said, "Anyone who has been turned down for a date has been a victim of the human drive to exert control over half the genes of one's future children."[5] To Pinker and others, genetic engineering does not threaten humanity's future, but rather offers a brighter one in which people have access to traits that allow them to be the best and healthiest versions of themselves. Australian ethicist Julian Savulescu, a leading voice in this field, even suggests humans have a moral obligation to do this. "We should give our children the greatest range of gifts possible," he argues. "Nature has no mind to fairness or equality."[6]

Whether genetic engineering poses a eugenic threat is one of the many topics debated in *Introducing Issues with Opposing Viewpoints: Genetic Engineering*. Students will also consider arguments about whether it is ethical to create designer babies or savior siblings, or to use genetic engineering to treat disease. How genetic engineering should be applied to plants and animals is considered, too, in opposing pairs that debate whether genetically modified food can alleviate world hunger and protect the environment, or whether it poses a health threat. Guided reading questions and challenging essay prompts encourage students to develop their own opinions on this twenty-first-century topic.

## Notes

1. Chuck Colson, "The Eliminators," Townhall.com, August 3, 2006. http://townhall.com/columnists/chuckcolson/2006/08/03/the_eliminators/page/full.

2. Colson, "The Eliminators."

3. Ronald Bailey, "Transhumanism: The Most Dangerous Idea?," *Reason,* August 25, 2004. http://reason.com/archives/2004/08/25 /transhumanism-the-most-dangero/1.

4. Bailey, "Transhumanism: The Most Dangerous Idea?"

5. Steven Pinker, "Better Babies? Why Genetic Enhancement Is Too Unlikely to Worry About," *Boston Globe,* June 1, 2003.

6. Julian Savulescu, "Breeding Perfect Babies," Australian Broadcasting Company, November 12, 2008. www.abc.net.au /unleashed/37548.html.

# Chapter 1

# Is Genetic Engineering Ethical?

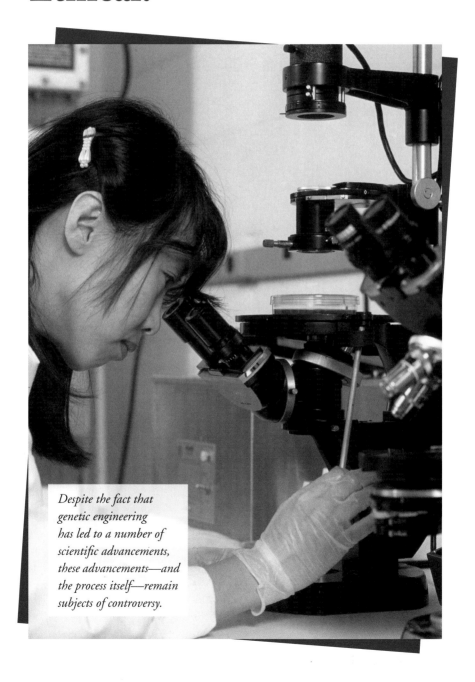

*Despite the fact that genetic engineering has led to a number of scientific advancements, these advancements—and the process itself—remain subjects of controversy.*

# Genetic Engineering Is Ethical

> *"None of us chooses our own genes. What is the moral significance in the fact that our genes were imposed on us due to someone's choice as opposed to just chance?"*

## Bonnie Steinbock

In the following viewpoint Bonnie Steinbock argues that genetic engineering is moral and rational. She contends that determining traits and talents via genetic engineering is not much different from the process of choosing a certain type of partner with whom to mate or choosing which skills, talents, and interests one will nurture in their children. She rejects claims that genetic engineering would foster social inequalities. In Steinbock's opinion, society is rife with inequality anyway, and genetic engineering could actually help poorer members of society overcome their disadvantages. Steinbock concludes there is no moral reason to oppose genetic engineering. She thinks genetic interventions stand to improve people and society and do not differ much from other forms of influence and selection already practiced by parents.

Steinbock specializes in bioethics. She is a professor of philosophy at the State University of New York at Albany.

1. Who is Steven Pinker and how does he factor into the author's argument?
2. According to Steinbock, why is there no difference between people who naturally inherit a gene that predisposes them to cheerfulness and people who would be genetically engineered to possess it?
3. Why is genetic engineering not a form of "parental tyranny," according to Steinbock?

The phrase "designer babies" refers to genetic interventions into pre-implantation embryos in the attempt to influence the traits the resulting children will have. At present, this is not possible, but many people are horrified by the mere thought that parents might want to choose their children's genes, especially for non-disease traits. I want to argue that the objections are usually not well articulated, and that even when they are, it's far from obvious that such interventions would be wrong.

What precisely is the objection? Of course, there are safety objections, especially ones arising from unforeseen and harmful side-effects. For example, in mice, researchers have shown that the addition of a certain gene made them better at running mazes, but also made them hyper-sensitive to pain. Such a possibility would rule out most, if not all, genetic enhancement. However, safety objections are raised by all new technologies, and do not usually instigate calls for blanket prohibition. The interesting question is, assuming genetic enhancement of the embryo is safe and effective, may such techniques ethically be used by parents?

## All Parents Influence Their Children's Traits

Do the critics base their opposition on a general objection to the attempt to influence children's traits? Surely not. That is exactly what parents are supposed to do. To get our children to be healthy, well mannered, intellectually curious, and well behaved we control what they eat, have them vaccinated, teach them manners, read to them, and discipline them when they misbehave. It would be absurd for a

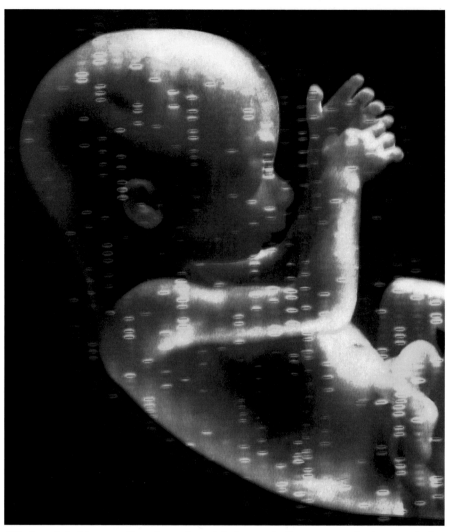

*"Designer baby" is a term for embryos that might be genetically programmed to have particular genetic traits, such as a desirable eye or hair color.*

parent to say, "I never attempt to influence my children's development. I just love them for who they are." Thus, it is not influencing our children's traits that is objectionable, but rather the means to accomplish this, that is, choosing their genes. But even this has to be further refined, since just the choice of a partner—surely not morally objectionable in itself—is a way of choosing our children's genes. As [Harvard psychology professor] Steven Pinker has put it, "Anyone who has been turned down for a date has been a victim of the human drive to exert control over half the genes of one's future children."

Perhaps the objection is not to exerting control over traits, but rather to completely determining in advance what traits one's children will or will not have. Genetic interventions, it may be thought, enable more control over what our children will be like than other modes of shaping children. If this is the objection, it embodies the "fallacy of genetic determinism," the view that our genes determine who we are and what we are like. Of course genes play a role in the traits we have, but what we are actually like is the result of multiple genes interacting with each other, and all of them interacting with the environment. In fact, even if you could choose the entire genome of a child (for example, by cloning), you would not have complete control over the child's traits. As Princeton microbiologist Lee Silver has put it, "All that anyone will ever get from the use of cloning, or any other reproductive technology, is an unpredictable son or daughter, who won't listen to his parents any more than my children will listen to me." Thus, the very term "designer babies" is a misnomer. No one will ever be able to design a child, that is, determine in advance what talents, skills, abilities, virtues, and vices the child will have.

## No More Chosen and No Less Human

Perhaps the objection is to the fact that the child's genes were chosen for him by his parents, thus forcing the child to have certain talents and not others. For example, it might be thought that if the child's parents picked genes associated with musical ability, their child would be forced to be a musician, when maybe he or she would rather have been an athlete. But this makes no sense. Consider a child of musicians who inherits musical ability naturally. That child may become a musician, but he or she certainly isn't forced to do so because of his genetic inheritance. Far from it; if the child doesn't practice, he won't become a musician, no matter what his genetic make-up. Admittedly, when parents choose their children's genes, they do so without the child's knowledge and consent. However, this is true of all of us, not just those who are genetically modified. None of us chooses our own genes. What is the moral significance in the fact that our genes were imposed on us due to someone's choice as opposed to just chance?

Some people believe that genetically modified people would have personalities, thoughts, and feelings that would be less real, less authentic than the personalities of non-modified people. But this too makes no sense, as an example will reveal. In 2003, Avshalom Caspi and colleagues reported in *Science* that a functional polymorphism [the quality or state of existing in different forms] in the promoter region of the serotonin transporter (5-HTT) gene may be associated with a predisposition towards depression. Individuals with one or two copies of the short allele of the 5-HTT promoter polymorphism become depressed more often after stressful events than individuals homozygous for the long allele. So if you're lucky enough to have inherited two long alleles of 5-HTT, you may be more likely to be a cheerful, resilient sort of person than someone who inherited two short alleles. What if it were possible to genetically modify embryos to replace the short alleles with long ones? Would the resulting people not really be as cheerful or resilient as those who naturally inherited the long alleles? Of course not.

## Genetic Modification Would Not Change the Way People Parent

A more serious objection stems from the idea that people who want to choose, in advance, the traits their child will have, and are willing to spend so much money to get a child with certain traits, demonstrate a kind of desire for perfectionism that seems incompatible with being a good parent. An insistence on having a child of a certain sort, whether a musician or an athlete or a politician, amounts to parental tyranny. As [bioethicist] Thomas Murray has put the point, "When parents attempt to shape their children's characteristics to match their preferences and expectations, such an exercise of free choice on the parents' part may constrain their child's prospects for flourishing."

An argument related to parental tyranny has been made by a member of the US President's Council on Bioethics, Michael Sandel. Sandel suggests that genetic engineering threatens what he calls the "ethic of giftedness." He argues that "To appreciate our children as gifts is to accept them as they come, not as objects of our design or products of our will or instruments of our ambition." This notion of giftedness resonates with many people, because it represents an ideal of parenting that most of us embrace. Sandel contrasts the ethic of giftedness with a style of parenting he calls "hyper-parenting," which ignores the child's own talents and abilities, and instead forces the child to do what will satisfy parental dreams and aspirations. A hyper-parent might insist that a child play sports, when he or she would rather be in the drama club, or that all the child's free time be spent in pursuit of getting into a prestigious university. We can all agree that hyper-parents are obnoxious, but is there a necessary connection between hyper-parenting and interest in genetic modification of the embryo? No doubt many hyper-parents would be interested in genetically modifying their embryos, but it doesn't follow that everyone who would opt for genetic modification would be hyper-parents. That depends, I think, on the traits chosen, and the reasons for choosing them. If the traits sought were ones that could reasonably be thought to benefit the child, whatever path the child might choose, traits that would help a person flourish, traits that good parents would want to instill in their children anyway, such as kindness, generosity, compassion, or creativity, it is hard to see why choosing such traits, by genetic or conventional means, would be hyper-parenting.

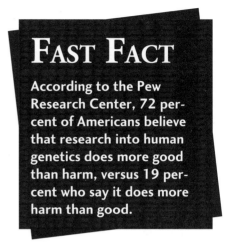

**FAST FACT**

According to the Pew Research Center, 72 percent of Americans believe that research into human genetics does more good than harm, versus 19 percent who say it does more harm than good.

## Genetic Engineering Could Fight Inequality

A final objection to "designer children" is that this would exacerbate social differences and the gap between rich and poor. I seriously doubt that genetic interventions would have more of an influence than existing causes of inequality, such as rotten neighbourhoods and lousy schools. In any event, prebirth genetic enhancement could be used to combat social inequality, by giving children from disadvantaged backgrounds a leg up.

Genetic enhancement of embryos is, for the present, science fiction. Its opponents think that we need to ban it now, before it ever becomes a reality. What they have not provided are clear reasons to agree. Their real opposition is not to a particular means of shaping children, but rather to a certain style of parenting. Rather than [fetishising] the technology, the discussion should focus on which parental attitudes and modes of parenting help children to flourish. It may be that giving children "genetic edges" of certain kinds would not constrain their lives and choices, but actually make them better. That possibility should not be dismissed out of hand.

## EVALUATING THE AUTHOR'S ARGUMENTS:

Bill Muehlenberg, author of the following viewpoint, thinks genetic engineering is immoral because it allows humans to "play God." How do you think the author of this viewpoint, Bonnie Steinbock, would respond to his argument? After writing a few sentences about what she might say, state with which perspective you agree.

# Genetic Engineering Is Unethical

**Bill Muehlenberg**

> *"The fact that nature deals us all an uneven hand is no argument for genetic manipulation, selection and the creation of a perfect race."*

In the following viewpoint Bill Muehlenberg argues that the contemporary fascination with genetic engineering may be more a cause for concern than a panacea for all our ills. He begins by looking at some specific issues involving Australian bioethicists, noticing how traditional ethics may be short-changed by their various proposals. He then takes a broader look at the mixed blessings of genetic engineering. He asks whether seeking to create perfect humans may in fact result in more harm than good and suggests that such God-like powers may well come at a price. He reminds us of how recent historical attempts at seeking to do just this have produced disastrous results. In seeking to manufacture a perfect race, the temptation for those with the power to do so is to ride roughshod over basic human rights and freedoms. He warns of the dangers in reducing human beings merely to their genetic make-up and argues that we must proceed with caution in these areas. He says that good intentions alone are not enough. At risk is what it means to be human.

Bill Muehlenberg, "Those Unethical Ethicists," billmuehlenberg.com, November 11, 2008, www.billmuehlenberg.com.

Muehlenberg lectures in ethics in Australia and offers commentary on a wide range of social and ethical issues at his website, CultureWatch: http://www.billmuehlenberg.com/.

**AS YOU READ, CONSIDER THE FOLLOWING QUESTIONS:**
1. What does the word "reductionism" mean in the context of the viewpoint?
2. What, in Muehlenberg's opinion, is an appropriate way to deal with a genetic imperfection such as short-sightedness?
3. What is the problem with prolonging life, according to the author?

Why is it that Australia seems to produce so many "ethicists" who would perhaps have been perfectly at home in a certain European nation about 70 years ago (beginning with 'G' and ending with 'y'). Why do they so often seem to be advocates for the culture of death, and so very devoid of any respect for human life?

Think of some Australian ethicists, philosophers, and biomedical experts such as Peter Singer, or Alan Trounson, or Julian Savulescu. They are all prominent medical thinkers or practitioners, and all have a Brave New World feel about them.

Consider the recent remarks of Prof Savulescu. In an article entitled "Breeding perfect babies" he makes the case for genetic engineering and designer babies. He argues that "we have a moral obligation to select the embryo with the best chance of the best life". He says new developments in testing for genetic disease mean anyone can now pick and choose the characteristics they want for their baby.

He explains, "The (AU$3,440) test, called karyomapping, which should be available as early as next year, will allow couples at risk of passing on gene defects to conceive healthy children using IVF treatment. The 'genetic MoT' will transform the range of inherited disorders that can be detected. Currently only 2% of the 15,000 known genetic conditions can be detected in this way. Not only can it test for muscular dystrophy, cystic fibrosis and Huntington's disease, but it can be used for testing for the risk of developing heart disease, cancer, diabetes and Alzheimer's in later life."

Now it is one thing to think about screening for certain genetic diseases. But Savulescu is quite happy to take all this much further. "We should want our children to begin life with the best genetic start. People worry that this is a slide down a slope to creating designer babies, to testing for eye colour, height, mental and physical abilities. But we should embrace the selection of such non-disease traits, if they contribute to a child having a better chance of a better life. Why wouldn't we choose an embryo which will grow into a better ability at maths or music. Indeed, we should give our children the greatest range of gifts possible."

*Critics of genetic engineering say that the creation of designer babies puts scientists and doctors in a position to "play God."*

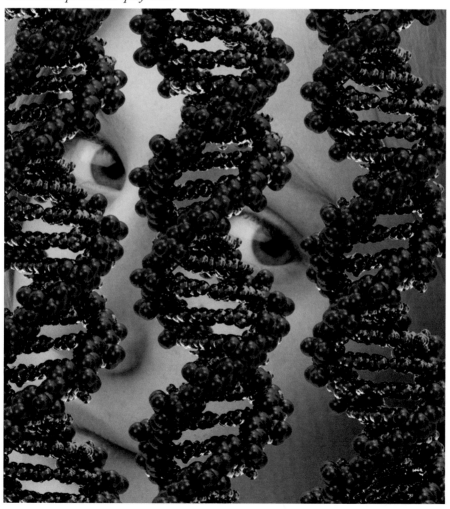

This is really all about creating designer babies who are made to order for adults with selective tastes. It is indeed about playing God, and determining just who is allowed to live, and who will not be allowed to live.

Yet Savulescu simply dismisses any ethical concerns people might have about all this: "People worry that this is like the Nazis weeding out the weak and inferior. Or that it will result in a two tiered society of the genetically privileged and the genetically underprivileged, as in the film *Gattaca*. But these fears are misplaced provided we focus on testing for genes that make our children's lives go predictably better. Nature has no mind to fairness or equality. Some people are born with horribly short genetic straws. Enabling couples to choose the best of the embryos will reduce natural inequality."

But what he is proposing is exactly the stuff of Nazi Germany and *Gattaca*. It is all about the creation of a superior race, based on genetics and selective breeding. Too bad about those who won't be able to afford all this high-biotech utopia. They will simply become the genetic underclass that *Gattaca* so rightly warns about.

And the fact that nature deals us all an uneven hand is no argument for genetic manipulation, selection and the creation of a perfect race. This is problematic for numerous reasons. Let me mention just a few.

A major problem is this: what do parents do with all the genetic information provided by the doctor? The truth is, many of the diseases tested for have no known cures at present. So the usual solution is that the doctor advises an abortion. Indeed, many doctors and clinics will not do genetic testing unless the couple gives prior consent to having an abortion.

But as ethicist Anthony Fisher reminds us, scientists should focus on curing such diseases rather than eliminating people with the con-

# "Designing" One's Baby Is Unethical

A majority of Britons polled think that parents should not be able to pick and choose their children's traits for any reason.

**Question:**
"Now that we have the technology to modify an embryo's genes, should we allow parents the freedom to design their own babies?"

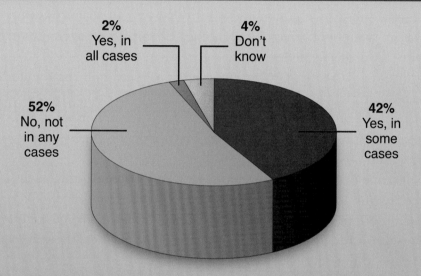

2%
Yes, in all cases

4%
Don't know

52%
No, not in any cases

42%
Yes, in some cases

Taken from: YouGov/*Spectator* poll, February 21–24, 2006.

dition. Genetic screening can easily lead to selective breeding and selective abortion. It can easily lead us to a return to eugenics.

## Genetic Reductionism

But there may be even greater problems to worry about here. It seems that the very notions of human rights and human dignity come under threat here. The new genetics is in many ways related to the reductionism of the human person. That is, the more we come to know about the human genome, the more we are tempted to explain everything in terms of genetics. While we certainly can be understood in part by our genetic makeup, we are more than the sum of our genes. Bioethicist Leon Kass puts it this way:

"One of the most worrisome but least appreciated aspects of the godlike power of the new genetics is its tendency to 'redefine' a human being in terms of his genes. Once a person is decisively characterized by his genotype, it is but a short step to justifying death solely for genetic sins."

Not only is this whole process dehumanising, but it means that certain technocrats will be making decisions which will have huge moral and social ramifications. As C.S. Lewis warned with great prescience years ago in *The Abolition of Man*: "What we call Man's power over Nature turns out to be power exercised by some men over other men with Nature as its instrument."

He went on to say, "Man's conquest of Nature, if the dreams of some scientific planners are realized, means the rule of a few hundreds of men over billions upon billions of men. There neither is nor can be any simple increase of power on Man's side. Each new power won *by* man is a power *over* man as well."

No one denies that nature deals us a bad hand at times, and there certainly is a place for taking steps to correct some of this. People born short-sighted obviously can make use of corrective prescription glasses. And there may well be a place for genetic testing for certain diseases and defects.

But the whole enterprise is fraught with danger, and the desire to move on to designer babies, complete with improved musical and mathematical abilities—as Savulescu desires—is surely putting us on the wrong road. Indeed, we have travelled down that road before, and it has not been a pretty sight.

The path to a coercive utopia is often paved with good intentions. We all want to live longer and healthier lives. But as Leon Kass reminds us, "It is not just *survival*, but survival of *what* that matters. . . . [S]imply to covet a prolonged life span for ourselves is both a sign and a cause of our failure to open ourselves to this—or any other—purpose. It is probably no accident that it is a generation whose intelligentsia proclaim the meaningless of life that embarks on its indefinite prolongation and that seeks to cure the emptiness of life by extending it."

Quite so. As we increasingly lose our understanding of what it is to be human, and what is really important in life, we increasingly look to play God, either to extend our own physical lives, or that of our offspring. But there are right ways and wrong ways of doing this. Denying God, and/or seeking to take His place is not the right way to proceed.

## EVALUATING THE AUTHOR'S ARGUMENTS:

Bill Muehlenberg argues there are moral types of physical enhancements, such as wearing glasses or braces, and immoral kinds of physical enhancements, such as those that would occur on the genetic level. What do you think? Do you think there is a significant difference between wearing contact lenses and genetically engineering a person to have perfect vision? Why or why not? Is one more moral than the other, in your opinion? Explain your reasoning.

**Viewpoint**

**3**

# It Is Ethical to Genetically Engineer Children for Non-disease Traits

**Julian Savulescu**

*"We need not fear perfection."*

In the following viewpoint Julian Savulescu argues that not only should humans genetically engineer people to be disease free, but they should also select for non-disease traits such as appearance, intelligence, memory, talent, and other qualities. In his opinion, limiting genetic science to disabilities and diseases is wrong: Parents have a moral obligation to provide their children with the best life possible, and that includes offering them the highest-quality talents, skills, and physical features. If humans should one day be able to create superior people, then they should absolutely do so, says Savulescu. He believes that genetic engineering eliminates the cruel inconsistencies of nature and fosters equality by offering the same abilities to everyone. He concludes that engineering the best possible babies is both ethical and rational.

Savulescu is a professor at the Oxford Uehiro Centre for Practical Ethics at the University of Oxford in the United Kingdom.

**AS YOU READ, CONSIDER THE FOLLOWING QUESTIONS:**
1. What does Savulescu say all parents should strive to give their children?
2. According to Savulescu, what will prevent society from becoming split into two classes of people (those who are genetically privileged and those who are genetically underprivileged)?
3. Why will humans never achieve perfection, according to Savulescu?

Prospective parents will be able to screen embryos for almost any known genetic disease using a revolutionary "universal test" developed by British scientists, led by Prof Alan Handyside. The (AU$3,440) test, called karyomapping, which should be available as early as next year [2009], will allow couples at risk of passing on gene defects to conceive healthy children using IVF [in vitro fertilization] treatment. The "genetic MoT" will transform the range of inherited disorders that can be detected. Currently only 2% of the 15,000 known genetic conditions can be detected in this

*A human embryo is genetically screened prior to being implanted in a uterus. Embryos can be tested for genetic predisposition to disease, as well as for genes that contribute to various mental and physical characteristics.*

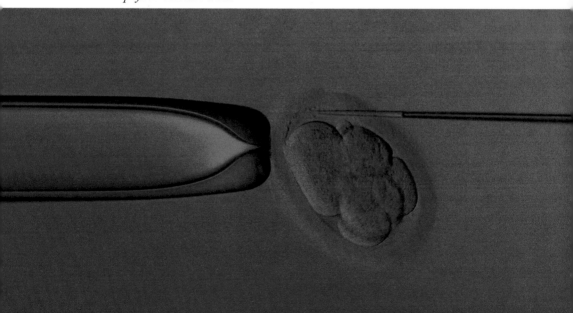

way. Not only can it test for muscular dystrophy, cystic fibrosis and Huntington's disease, but it can be used for testing for the risk of developing heart disease, cancer, diabetes and Alzheimer's in later life.

Such Preimplantation Genetic Screening of embryos could be used not just to test for the genetic predisposition to disease, but also for genes which contribute to intelligence, personality type (neurotic, extroverted, etc.), memory, impulse control, perfect pitch, and, in general, the genetic contribution to our physical and mental abilities, and disabilities.

I have argued that we have a moral obligation to select the embryo with the best chance of the best life. This brings us one step closer to being able to do that.

## We Should Want Our Children to Have the Best Traits

The HFEA [Human Fertilisation and Embryo Authority] currently limits genetic testing to severe genetic disorders. But such limits are wrong and irrational. Imagine a couple has two embryos that are free of major genetic disorders. A has a 10% chance of Alzheimer Disease while B does not. What possible reason could there be NOT to select B? Why would we leave it to chance?

People will of course choose to select out first the worst conditions but why shouldn't we have a child with no risk of Alzheimer's Disease, rather than one with a risk, even if that risk is small. We should want our children to begin life with the best genetic start.

People worry that this is a slide down a slope to creating designer babies, to testing for eye colour, height, mental and physical abilities. But we should embrace the selection of such non-disease traits, if they contribute to a child having a better chance of a better life. Why wouldn't we choose an embryo that

> **FAST FACT**
>
> Geneticist David Goldstein of Duke University in North Carolina has predicted that by 2020 researchers will have discovered genetic variations that cause diabetes, heart disease, and psychiatric disorders, and it will be possible to detect these in embryos. He thinks this will dramatically increase parents' interest in genetically engineering their children.

# Americans Think Genetic Testing Has Changed Society for the Better

A 2009 poll by the Pew Research Center found that the majority of Americans thought genetic testing had changed society for the better, though not to as great a degree as cell phones, green products, e-mail, and the Internet.

## "Which of the following developments has been a change for the better, a change for the worse, or hasn't this made much difference?"

| Development | Change for the better | Change for the worse | Not much difference | Unsure |
|---|---|---|---|---|
| Cell phones | 69% | 14% | 11% | 5% |
| Environmentally conscious or "green" products | 68% | 7% | 22% | 3% |
| E-mail | 65% | 7% | 19% | 9% |
| The Internet | 65% | 16% | 11% | 8% |
| Increasing racial and ethnic diversity | 61% | 9% | 25% | 5% |
| Increasing surveillance and security measures | 58% | 17% | 21% | 3% |
| Handheld devices such as BlackBerrys and iPhones | 56% | 25% | 12% | 7% |
| Online shopping | 54% | 15% | 24% | 8% |
| More choices in news and entertainment | 54% | 16% | 27% | 3% |
| **Genetic testing** | **53%** | **13%** | **22%** | **13%** |
| Increasing acceptance of gays and lesbians | 38% | 28% | 28% | 6% |
| Social networking sites, such as Facebook | 35% | 21% | 31% | 12% |
| Cable news talk and opinion shows | 34% | 30% | 31% | 5% |
| More people having money in the stock market | 31% | 34% | 26% | 9% |
| Internet blogs | 29% | 21% | 36% | 14% |
| Reality TV shows | 8% | 63% | 22% | 7% |
| More people getting tattoos | 7% | 40% | 45% | 8% |

Figures are approximate, due to rounding.

Taken from: Pew Research Center poll, December 9–13, 2009.

will grow into a better ability at maths or music. Indeed, we should give our children the greatest range of gifts possible.

## Genetic Engineering Makes People Equal

People worry that this is like the Nazis weeding out the weak and inferior. Or that it will result in a two tiered society of the genetically privileged and the genetically underprivileged, as in the film *Gattaca*.

But these fears are misplaced provided we focus on testing for genes that make our children's lives go predictably better. Nature has no mind to fairness or equality. Some people are born with horribly short genetic straws. Enabling couples to choose the best of the embryos will reduce natural inequality.

And it is already relatively cheap. The cost of this kind of technology is falling exponentially. It will in the foreseeable future be as common as ultrasound in pregnancy.

Does this mean that we will create the perfect baby?

## We Have an Obligation to Choose Genetically Superior Children

Firstly, with the current numbers of embryos available in IVF, we can only test for two or three conditions. You will have to choose between testing for risk of heart disease or hair colour. Parents should test for those conditions that have the greatest impact on their children's wellbeing.

However, in the foreseeable future, this barrier of embryo number (up to about 20) may be overcome. For example, we could clone a woman's skin cell, or genetically modify it directly to produce stem cells. These stems could be used to produce eggs. In this way, we could use stem cell technology to produce hundreds of thousands of eggs from one skin cell from one woman. This would enable the production of hundreds of thousands of embryos and testing using this current technology for *many more* genetic conditions, including perhaps dispositions to mental and physical abilities.

Many steps in this process of producing egg from stem cells are complete in experiments in animals and raise many profound ethical issues. One of these is that, coupled with Preimplantation Genetic Screening, we would select embryos from a couple that would be more genetically privileged than any they would have likely produced naturally.

## We Need Not Fear Perfection

Does this mean that we will be able to make the perfect baby? No. There are many other influences besides genes that determine how good our lives are. There are maternal factors in pregnancy, the environmental and familial and peer influences. No matter how good the genetic start of our children is in life, they will never be perfect. And even if they were, life is risky and differences and deficiencies and disabilities would quickly emerge just as we lived life.

We need not fear perfection. We will never have it. Selecting the best is far short of selecting the perfect.

**EVALUATING THE AUTHOR'S ARGUMENTS:**

Julian Savulescu believes that all parents are obligated to give their children the best chance they can in life. Therefore, he thinks it is moral to genetically engineer people for non-disease traits, such as appearance and skill, because these are qualities that contribute to a person's overall success. Allen Goldberg, the author of the following viewpoint, disagrees, saying these are superficial traits that are neither important nor ethical to engineer. After reading both viewpoints, with which author do you agree? Why? What piece of evidence or line of reasoning swayed you?

# Viewpoint 4

# Genetic Engineering Is Only Ethical If It Improves Health

**Allen Goldberg**

*"Abusing . . . hard-won knowledge to capriciously choose hair color, eye color and other cosmetic traits in a baby is wrong and repugnant."*

In this viewpoint Allen Goldberg uses the story of his son, Henry, to illustrate why he thinks it is unethical to use genetic engineering for anything but the treatment of disease. Goldberg discusses how he and his wife used genetic engineering techniques to try to save the life of their son, who suffered from a rare genetic disease that ultimately killed him. Goldberg is upset that the techniques used to help Henry could be offered to parents so they can select for superficial traits like eye and hair color. Goldberg thinks this is wrong, disrespectful, and immoral. In his opinion, genetic engineering should be reserved for treating or eradicating the kinds of life-threatening illnesses that killed his son, not for picking and choosing shallow cosmetic characteristics. He concludes that using genetic engineering to design cosmetically perfect babies threatens to undermine the credibility of the entire scientific endeavor.

**AS YOU READ, CONSIDER THE FOLLOWING QUESTIONS:**
  1. What is preimplantation genetic diagnosis, as described by the author?
  2. What is Fanconi anemia, according to Goldberg?
  3. When did Goldberg's son, Henry, die?

Something stinks about reproductive medicine in Southern California, and it doesn't involve eight dirty diapers.[1]

## Creating Designer Babies Is Wrong

Recently [in 2009], the Los Angeles–based Fertility Institutes announced that it would soon be offering patients at its clinics the chance to choose traits such as "eye color, hair color and complexion." The clinics already offer gender selection to patients undergoing in vitro fertilization.

The Fertility Institutes employs a technique known as "preimplantation genetic diagnosis [PGD]," which allows doctors to screen embryos soon after they are created in a petri dish and implant only the ones that meet certain criteria. The technique was invented to help high-risk families avoid or manage potentially deadly genetic traits, and to help women who've had multiple miscarriages conceive babies they can carry to term.

Now the Fertility Institutes is corrupting this lifesaving clinical procedure by using it to help families create designer babies, and I worry that their excesses will turn public sentiment against all preimplantation genetic diagnosis. That would be wrong.

## Genetic Engineering Should Be Reserved for Treating Serious Diseases

My son, Henry, was born with a rare and fatal genetic disease, Fanconi anemia. Fanconi patients are born with faulty immune systems and a

---

1. A reference to Nadya Suleman, also known as "Octomom," an American mother of six who in 2009 gave birth to octuplets conceived through in vitro fertilization.

Americans' support for reproductive genetic testing depends heavily on the circumstances for which it is being used. The majority approve of testing for health-related problems but not for choosing traits such as eye color or intelligence.

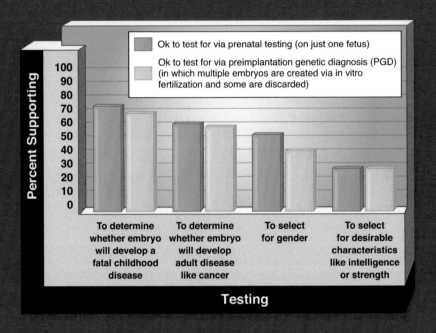

Taken from: Genetics and Public Policy Center, "Reproductive Genetic Testing: What America Thinks," 2004.

host of health problems. They are at high risk for leukemia and other deadly diseases and usually die before the age of 30. The only hope is a bone marrow transplant that replaces the immune systems they are born with. The transplants are most likely to succeed if the donor is a sibling who is a perfect genetic match.

My wife, Laurie, and I had always planned to have more children, and in the late 1990s we decided to try to employ preimplantation genetic diagnosis in an attempt to conceive a baby free of the deadly disease who would be a perfectly matched cord-blood donor for

Henry. Cord blood is usually disposed of after birth, and harvesting it causes no problems or discomfort for a baby.

We were among the first families attempting the technique, but after three years of trying unsuccessfully, we ran out of time. Henry's health was deteriorating, and he needed an immediate transplant, which he got from an unrelated donor. Ultimately, his body rejected it. In December 2002, he died at the age of 7.

In the decade since we first tried to conceive using embryo screening, the technology has improved and has saved many lives. I get letters and e-mails with regularity from other Fanconi anemia families who were able to conceive babies who saved their siblings' lives.

But not all Fanconi families are lucky enough to live in the United States, where preimplantation genetic diagnosis is legal. The regulation and availability of the technique in the European Union is a patchwork, and some countries ban the practice outright.

## FAST FACT

According to researchers at the University of Liverpool, today's reproductive scientists regularly use preimplantation genetic diagnosis to identify 170 different conditions, including cystic fibrosis and hemoglobin disorders.

## It Is Immoral to Waste Science on Cosmetic Selection

I understand that there are ethical issues surrounding the procedure. Not all families are comfortable with creating embryos in the laboratory knowing that some of them will be discarded. And no one would advocate creating a child who is only wanted to save another's life. But the choice of whether to employ screening is a deeply personal one and should be considered with great care by families in consultation with their doctors and genetic counselors.

What I now fear, though, is that clinics offering trait selection to satisfy the whims of parents will turn people against a procedure that can save lives.

Henry was among the most optimistic, wise and courageous people I have ever met. We felt a great responsibility to do everything in our

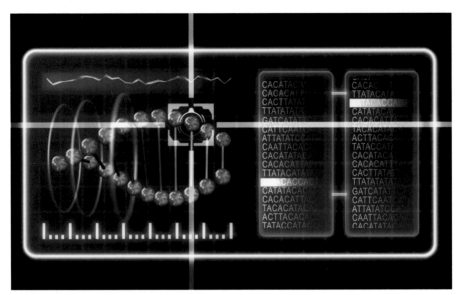

*A conceptual image of genetic screening shows genetic code (right) and a DNA molecule (left), in which a cursor tracks one of the DNA microspheres. The screening is used for preimplantation genetic diagnosis to test for genetic disorders.*

power to save his life. In the end, that wasn't possible. But our efforts contributed to scientific knowledge, and for that we are grateful. Abusing that hard-won knowledge to capriciously choose hair color, eye color and other cosmetic traits in a baby is wrong and repugnant.

## EVALUATING THE AUTHOR'S ARGUMENTS:

Instead of relying on facts, statistics, or historical examples the way other authors in this section do to make their arguments, Allen Goldberg, the author of this viewpoint, focuses on the narrative story of his son, who died of a rare genetic blood disorder. In what ways does the narrative style differ from that of the other authors? What advantages and disadvantages might there be in describing one person's personal story? Explain your answer and state whether you agree with Goldberg that genetic engineering should be limited to treating disease.

**Viewpoint**

**5**

# It Is Ethical to Genetically Engineer a Child to Save a Sibling's Life

**Caroline Davies**

*"He is a saviour sibling, and he's very proud of that."*

In the following viewpoint Caroline Davies, a reporter for the British newspaper the *Guardian*, reports on a family who genetically engineered one of their children to save the life of his brother. Davies explains that Charlie Whitaker was born with a rare blood disorder that threatened his life. Aside from painful and frequent blood transfusions, the only cure was to use the cord blood from a sibling who was an exact tissue match. Cord blood is taken from the umbilical cord at birth and its extraction does not harm the baby who has just been born. After failing to naturally conceive a child who was a match for Charlie, the Whitakers used genetic engineering techniques to have a baby, named Jamie, whose blood was guaranteed to be Charlie's exact match. The Whitakers reject claims they have created life only to save life; they argue their sons have a unique bond and that Jamie is proud that he helped save his brother. In their opinion, it would have been unethical to let Charlie die, and they argue they love all their children equally and do not treat Jamie as a biological servant. They conclude there is everything right about using genetic engineering techniques to have a baby who can offer lifesaving cells for a sibling.

**AS YOU READ, CONSIDER THE FOLLOWING QUESTIONS:**
1. What is Diamond Blackfan anemia and how is it typically treated?
2. What were the Whitakers' chances of having two babies with Diamond Blackfan anemia?
3. What does Davies say bonds brothers Jamie and Charlie?

Michelle Whitaker visibly winces at the term designer baby. "Horrible," she says. "Like 'harvest baby' or 'spare parts baby'. It's just wrong.

"What did we design about Jamie? Not his eye colour, his hair colour, his IQ, his height."

## "Saviour Siblings" Should Be Proud
So what about the term "saviour sibling"?

"Well, he is a saviour sibling, and he's very proud of that," she says, watching her youngest child playing in their Derbyshire back garden. Jamie celebrated his sixth birthday last week, a joyous occasion marked by a party at Laser Quest with his brother, Charlie, 10, sister Emily, seven, and friends.

Such normality contrasts greatly with the day he was born, delivered in the midst of raging controversy over embryo testing. Chosen through pre-implantation genetic diagnosis (PIGD) as a perfect tissue match for Charlie, who had been diagnosed with rare Diamond Blackfan anaemia [DBA], the method of Jamie's conception and birth was condemned by some campaigners as another step along a "stem cell-paved road to hell." . . .

It is hard to believe that now, as their three children scramble excitedly around the garden of their family home, a renovated cottage near Chesterfield with breathtaking views across the countryside, with their pet labrador and terrier in tow. Dinner is on. Notes pinned to the kitchen noticeboard testify to a busy life of Scouts, dentist's appointments, homework to be done, party invitations—the normal, semi-chaotic life enjoyed by millions of families throughout Britain.

## A Heartbreaking Beginning

But it didn't used to be like that. Looking at photographs, Michelle and Jayson can now see that Charlie was not a normal newborn. "He looks grey," says Michelle, though as a first-time mother she thought, perhaps, this was what he was supposed to look like.

It was not until he was 12 weeks that Diamond Blackfan anaemia, a life-threatening disease that stops the body producing red blood cells, was diagnosed. They were told: "Your child has DBA. This is the prognosis. This is the treatment. Go away and think about it."

But the prognosis was uncertain. Few in Britain had experience of it. Jayson found himself on the phone for hours to parents of sufferers in America. As for treatment, it would mean a lifetime of blood transfusions—one every three weeks—plus daily injections of Desferal, a drug to prevent the iron overload from transfusions

damaging his vital organs. "This can't be it," Jayson protested at the time. "It can't just be transfusions for the rest of his life. There must be something we can do."

"I cried my eyes out. I really did. I thought, 'Why us? Why not somebody else?' I was heartbroken," says Michelle.

So began a reality far removed from their dreams of parenthood. Charlie spent more time in hospital than out. Apart from the transfusions, he was regularly admitted with infections. Then there were the daily injections. "We had to stick a needle in his stomach every night, and hook him up to a pump for 12 hours," says Michelle. "I couldn't do it. Jayson did it, because he was stronger. And as Charlie got older and started talking, he would be crying: 'Please don't hurt me. You don't love me. Why are you hurting me?' I just couldn't cope with that."

## A Transplant Is the Only Hope

One consultant seemed to offer hope. There could be a cure, they were told, but it would involve a transplant. The trouble was, Charlie had no siblings. The Whitakers had always wanted a large family. "Five," they chime. Today, they have four—three of their own and a little girl they are fostering. But back then, there were concerns. They wondered if they could be carriers of a gene that causes DBA. They weren't. The cause of Charlie's illness was not genetic but a "sporadic mutation". Their chances of having another DBA baby were one in 50. They decided to risk it and conceived Emily naturally.

It was just before Emily was born that they heard of the case of Molly Nash, a girl from Minnesota born with Fanconi anaemia, an often fatal genetic disease, whose parents' decision to choose a "tissue-match" embryo as their second child—a sibling to help cure her—caused a global media sensation.

Just in case, the Whitakers decided to have Emily's cord blood stored. In the end, she turned out not to be a perfect match, but any disappointment was overwhelmed by the sheer relief that she was not suffering from DBA.

## "He Knows How He Was Made, and Why"

At around the same time, the Human Fertilisation and Embryology Authority (HFEA) was testing the water on embryo selection. In the first decision of its kind, it had given the go-ahead to Raj and Shahana Hashmi, from Leeds, to use PIGD to have a baby that would help cure their son, Zain, who was born with the blood disorder beta thalassaemia.

The decision provoked outrage from some quarters. Josephine Quintavalle, from Comment on Reproductive Ethics, successfully sued the HFEA for acting unlawfully, though that ruling was overturned in the court of appeal and by the law lords.

So it was against this backdrop that the Whitakers approached Dr Mohamed Taranissi, a leading fertility specialist, for help. But, while

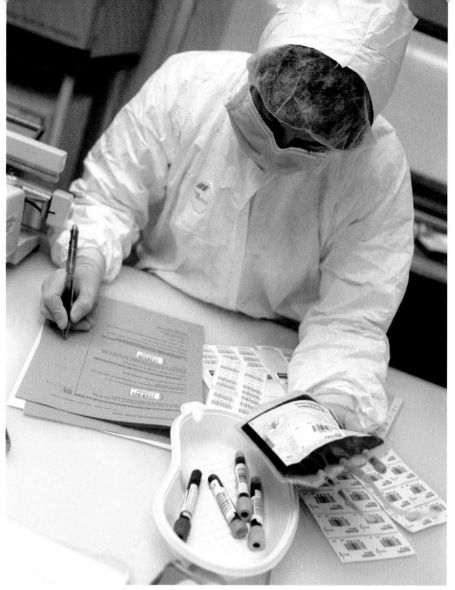

*Cord blood is collected from an umbilical cord following birth.*

he agreed, the HFEA said no. Jayson believes the HFEA's decision was swayed by the legal battle over the Hashmi family. "They wouldn't listen to us. They wouldn't listen to our specialists, even though we begged them." They refused the application on the grounds that, as Charlie's DBA was not genetic, the embryo itself would not benefit from screening.

The Whitakers responded by boarding a plane for Chicago. "There was lots of debate when Jamie was born, that he's going to be totally screwed up in the head because he's a 'saviour sibling', a 'spare parts'

# It Is Ethical to Create Savior Siblings

The majority of Americans think it is ethical to use genetic engineering techniques to birth a child with DNA that matches a sick sister or brother. More than 70 percent think it is moral to use prenatal testing to determine whether a fetus is a match. More than 60 percent think it is moral to use preimplantation genetic diagnosis (PGD) to do so. PGD is more controversial because it involves creating multiple embryos via in vitro fertilization, screening these for a DNA match, and discarding mismatches.

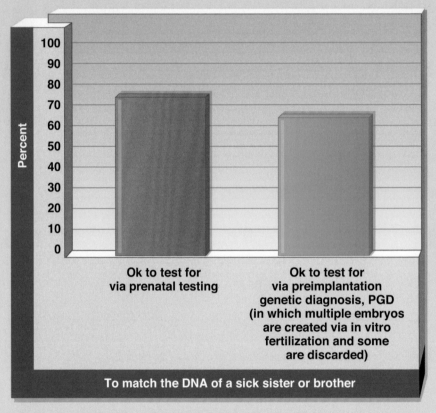

Taken from: Genetics and Public Policy Center, "Reproductive Genetic Testing: What America Thinks," 2004.

baby. It's all rubbish," says Michelle. "It's how you go about bringing a child up. We say to him he should have 'Made in America' tattooed on his bottom. He knows how he was made, and why he was made."

With the HFEA's refusal, the genetic screening and implantation of a tissue-match embryo was performed in America where the rules were more relaxed. But, with just a three-week window (they had to be back in Britain for Charlie's transfusions), and flying to the US with two small children and a box full of needles and medicine immediately after the 11 September attacks, it was an ordeal. Then, when Jamie was born the family had to wait 12 months in case he, too, showed symptoms of DBA.

## A Life Saved by a Sibling

Five years after his transplant, Charlie is still clear of DBA. And the bond between the two brothers is clear. "If anything, it's Emily, not Jamie, who feels left out, because she couldn't help," says Michelle.

Tucking into her roast chicken dinner, Emily proffers shyly: "Jamie says that Charlie needed boys' blood, that's why."

"No," counters Jamie. "He needed a match. It was easy-peasy," he adds. . . .

"We didn't have any hate mail, but people thought we were actually taking Jamie's bone marrow and bits of Jamie. It was just the cord blood that was required. Nothing else. It's a waste product thrown out at birth.

"It never crossed my mind that we would have to use Jamie again, and it was never mentioned to us, either."

Even if Charlie were to have a relapse? "Well, I don't know," she admits. "But that wouldn't be our decision. It would be up to the courts.

**EVALUATING THE AUTHOR'S ARGUMENTS:**

In the following viewpoint Wesley J. Smith argues that savior siblings like Jamie are, to some degree, treated as objects—and that conceiving children for utilitarian purposes raises serious ethical issues. How do you think the Whitakers would respond to this claim? Write one paragraph on what you think they might say. Then, state with which perspective you agree more: Is the creation of "savior siblings" ethical? Why or why not?

**Viewpoint 6**

# It Is Not Ethical to Genetically Engineer a Child to Save a Sibling's Life

*"What will happen when, rather than wanting the child, the parents harvest the stem cells and then put the child up for adoption because their family is big enough already?"*

## Wesley J. Smith

In the following viewpoint Wesley J. Smith argues that "savior siblings" pose many ethical issues. He contends that such children were given life only to be used as objects. Smith believes that it is unethical to genetically engineer children as "savior siblings" because parents might begin to treat their children merely as genetic donors. He concludes strict regulations are needed to protect children from such treatment by desperate, emotional parents. Wesley J. Smith is an award-winning author.

**AS YOU READ, CONSIDER THE FOLLOWING QUESTIONS:**

1. What happens if embryos fail to meet genetic screening criteria?
2. What are some of the issues Smith argues could arise from producing "savior siblings"?
3. As stated in the article, in what country are babies being killed for stem cells?

A baby was born in France because his parents wanted to use his umbilical cord stem cells to treat the genetic disease of their existing children. From the story:

France's first so-called "saviour sibling" was born in a hospital in the Parisian suburb of Clamart in late January, doctors announced Tuesday. The baby, whose blood stem cells will help cure one of his siblings from a severe genetic blood disease, has also opened a new front in the bioethics debate in France. Born to parents of Turkish origin and named Umut Talha (Turkish for "our hope"), the child

*A young patient cuddles her four-week-old brother just before undergoing a procedure involving the stem cells taken from the infant's cord blood. The prospect of using one sibling's genetic material to treat another sibling is controversial.*

was conceived under circumstances that would have been unthinkable only a generation ago. Umut Talha's parents approached the hospital in Clamart a little more than a year ago with a serious problem: their two young children were both afflicted with an inherited blood disorder, Beta thalassemia, which requires monthly blood transfusions. The parents knew the hospital was one of only three in France that was developing a treatment for their children's illness.

An embryo was screened and genetically selected from an original group of 12 embryos. It was picked to ensure it did not carry the gene for Beta thalassemia, but also based on its compatibility with the sick siblings. Besides selecting an offspring that would be spared from the disorder, the parents hoped the future baby would also become a donor of the right kind of treatment cells.

In the end the boy was born disorder-free, and his cells were confirmed to be compatible with his older sister, now aged two. Doctors feel confident that Umut's sister will be cured with the cells from his discarded umbilical cord, and her monthly blood transfusions will be discontinued. The family have since returned to their home in southern France, but they plan to return to Clamart to undergo the same procedure to cure their other child, Umut's four-year-old brother.

This isn't the first savior sibling to be born, and so far all the new babies that were created as medicine have also been wanted and loved. But embryos were created and discarded as medical waste if they didn't meet the genetic screening.

## Savior Siblings as Objects

Beyond the embryo issue, I want to look more deeply at this issue. Savior siblings are created specifically as objects, at least to some degree, because they were brought into being for a purely utilitarian

"Congratulations! It's a saviour sibling," cartoon by Grizelda. www.CartoonStock.com.

purpose. That being so, *why should the practice stop with creating savior siblings who are also wanted children?* What will happen when, rather than wanting the child, the parents harvest the stem cells and then put the child up for adoption because their family is big enough already? How about sending the embryo to India via Federal Express, having it implanted in a rented uterus, as already occurs, and then after you get the stem cells, just not taking the child home? That already happens, too, if the child doesn't meet the parents' expectations. I don't see any brakes to that.

And what if the family didn't want the baby to be born at all, but paid a surrogate to gestate and abort after seven months for tissues? Do we even have the lexicon to condemn such a dehumanization anymore, much less prohibit it? Such things may already be happening in the Ukraine, where the BBC reports babies being killed for stem cells and the *Daily Mail* reported that women were being paid to get pregnant and abort for fetal stem cells to be used in beauty treatments. Hear the crickets?

We enter harrowing ethical paths via hard cases. Vital principles are tossed aside in the emotions of the moment. With this practice gaining speed, regulations need to be fashioned that look at the big picture before we confront difficult situations.

I am not holding my breath. If recent history teaches us anything, Oprah Culture has incapacitated our abilities to set any real limits. Alleviating suffering, which has a very malleable and subjective meaning today, justifies almost anything. We never say, this far and no farther—well, sometimes we do, but we never mean it.

## EVALUATING THE AUTHOR'S ARGUMENTS:

In this viewpoint Wesley J. Smith argues that the creation of savior siblings destroys life—the life of the discarded embryos that do not genetically match their sick sibling. In the previous viewpoint Caroline Davies suggests the creation of savior siblings enables life—the life of the sibling that is threatened by disease. After reading both viewpoints, what is your opinion on whether savior siblings create or destroy life? What pieces of evidence swayed you? List at least two in your answer.

# Chapter 2

# Should Society Embrace Genetically Engineered Food?

*Although critics contend that genetically engineered foods are unsafe, supporters say such foods help alleviate hunger and are environmentally friendly.*

**Viewpoint**

**1**

# Genetically Modified Crops Can Alleviate World Hunger

**Pamela Ronald**

*"To meet the appetites of the world's population without drastically hurting the environment requires a visionary new approach: combining genetic engineering and organic farming."*

In the following viewpoint Pamela Ronald argues that genetically modified crops are the best solution to world hunger. She explains that the world's population is growing exponentially, and feeding all of those people puts an enormous strain on crop production, land, and resources such as water. But crops can be engineered to need less water and land all the while producing more food per acre, according to Ronald. She also says genetically engineered crops are designed to resist pests, disease, drought, cold, and flooding, which both reduces the amount of pesticides that need to be used and protects against crop failure, a big problem in starving countries. Furthermore, engineered crops can be made more nutritious than traditional crops, which also helps fight world hunger. For all of these reasons, she concludes that

Pamela Ronald, "The Problem of What to Eat: What If Organic Farmers Joined Forces with Genetic Engineers?," *Conservation Magazine,* July/September 2008, vol 9, no. 3. Copyright © 2008 by Pamela Ronald. All rights reserved. Reproduced by permission.

genetically engineered crops play a vital role in fighting world hunger and boosting agricultural production.

Ronald is a professor of plant pathology at the University of California–Davis, where she studies the role that genes play in a plant's response to its environment. She heads a laboratory that has genetically engineered rice to withstand disease and flooding, both of which threaten crops in poor countries in Asia and Africa.

**AS YOU READ, CONSIDER THE FOLLOWING QUESTIONS:**

1. How many people are expected to inhabit the planet by 2050, according to Ronald?
2. How did a genetically engineered papaya plant save Hawaii's papaya industry, according to the author?
3. What is "golden rice" and how does it factor into the author's argument?

Beginning in 1997, an important change swept over cotton farms in northern China. By adopting new farming techniques, growers found they could spray far less insecticide over their fields. Within four years they had reduced their annual use of the poisonous chemicals by about 70,000 metric tons—almost as much as is used in the entire state of California each year. Cotton yields in the region climbed, and production costs fell. Strikingly, the number of insecticide-related illnesses among farmers in the region dropped to one-fourth of their previous level.

This story, which has been repeated around the world, is precisely the kind of triumph over chemicals that organic-farming advocates wish for. But the hero in this story isn't organic farming. It is genetic engineering.

## Genetic Engineering Will Meet the Challenges of the Future

The most important change embraced by the Chinese farmers was to use a variety of cotton genetically engineered to protect itself against insects. The plants carry a protein called Bt, a favorite insecticide of organic farmers because it kills pests but is nontoxic to mammals,

*Chinese farmers harvest a cotton crop. The Chinese have genetically engineered a variety of insect-resistant cotton strains to reduce the number of crops lost to pests.*

birds, fish, and humans. By 2001, Bt cotton accounted for nearly half the cotton produced in China.

For anyone worried about the future of global agriculture, the story is instructive. The world faces an enormous challenge: Its growing population demands more food and other crops, but standard commercial agriculture uses industrial quantities of pesticides and harms the environment in other ways. The organic farming movement has shown that it is possible to dramatically reduce the use of insecticides and that doing so benefits both farm workers and the environment. But organic farming also has serious limits—there are many pests and diseases that cannot be controlled using organic approaches, and organic crops are generally more expensive to produce and buy.

To meet the appetites of the world's population without drastically hurting the environment requires a visionary new approach: combining genetic engineering and organic farming. . . .

## A Valuable Tool

Despite tremendous growth in the past 15 years, organic farms still produce just a tiny fraction of our food; they account for less than three percent of all U.S. agriculture and even less worldwide. In contrast, during the same period, the use of genetically engineered crops has increased to the point where they represent 50 to 90 percent of the acreage where they are available. These include insect-resistant varieties of cotton and corn; herbicide-tolerant soybean, corn, and canola; and virus-resistant papaya.

After more than a decade of genetically engineered crops and more than 30 years of organic farming, we know that neither method alone is sufficient to solve the problems faced—and caused—by agriculture.

It is time to abandon the caricatures of genetic engineering that are popular among some consumers and activists and instead see it for what it is: a tool that can help the ecological farming revolution grow into a lasting movement with global impact.

## Genetically Engineered Crops Protect the Environment

By 2050, the number of people on Earth is expected to increase from the current 6.7 billion to 9.2 billion. To feed those people with current crop yields and farming practices, we will need to clear, fertilize, and spray vast amounts of wild land. Millions of birds and billions of beneficial insects will die from lost habitat and industrial pesticides, farm workers will be at increased risk for disease, and the public will lose billions of dollars as a consequence of environmental degradation. Clearly, there must be a better way to boost food production while minimizing its impact.

An alternative is to expand the number of organic farms which do not use synthetic pesticides and which thus support higher levels of biodiversity than conventional farms. Some organic farmers even retain patches of natural habitat on farms to provide shelter for wildlife. But at current crop yields, farming will still need to absorb huge amounts of additional land—land that is now home to wildlife and diverse ecosystems. A clear challenge for the next century is to develop more productive crops, not just better farming techniques, and genetic engineering has demonstrated great promise here.

# The World Is Growing Genetically Modified Food

Genetically modified crops are grown by 15.4 million farmers in 29 countries. In 2010 they planted 148 million hectares (365 million acres) of genetically modified crops in both developing and industrial nations.

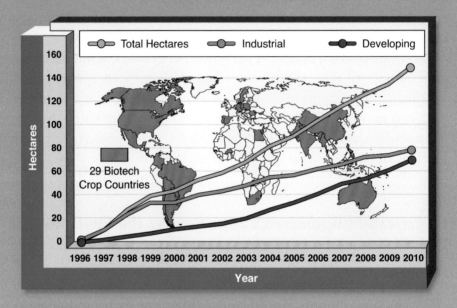

Taken from: Clive James, *ISAAA Report on Global Status of Biotech/GM Crops,* ISAAA Brief 42-2010, International Service for the Acquisition of Agri-Biotech Applications, 2010.

## Genetically Engineered Crops Are Hardy

One way to boost yields is to develop crops that can survive harsh conditions such as drought, cold, heat, salt, and flooding. Many of the world's poorest people farm in areas that are far from ideal, and freshwater sources are decreasing in quantity and quality throughout the world. Organic farming can help somewhat: Organically cultivated soil tends to hold water longer because of the higher levels of organic matter. Still, this approach has limits. Far more helpful would be new crop varieties designed to survive in difficult environments, and in the future this is where genetic engineering will likely have the most significant human and ecological impact. Crops with enhanced tolerance to drought, for instance, would allow farmers to produce more food using less water. Already there are varieties of genetically engineered wheat that can tolerate drought, as well as rice that can tolerate flooding and tomato plants that can tolerate salt.

## Genetically Engineered Crops Resist Pests and Disease

Another important challenge is to fight pests and disease, which take an estimated 20-to-40-percent bite out of agricultural productivity worldwide. Reducing this loss would be equivalent to creating more land and more water. But current pesticide use is a health and environmental hazard, and organic and genetic engineering offer complementary solutions. Genetic engineering can be used to develop seeds with enhanced resistance to pests and pathogens; organic farming can manage the overall spectrum of pests more effectively.

Genetically engineered crops have already enjoyed major success against pests. For example, in field trials carried out in central and southern India, where small-scale farmers typically suffer large losses because of pests, average yields of genetically engineered

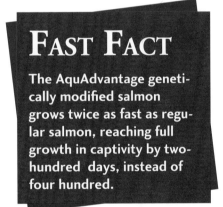

**FAST FACT**

The AquAdvantage genetically modified salmon grows twice as fast as regular salmon, reaching full growth in captivity by two-hundred days, instead of four hundred.

crops exceeded those of conventional crops by 80 percent. In Hawaii, the 1998 introduction of an engineered papaya plant that could resist the papaya ringspot virus virtually saved the industry. There was no organic approach available then to protect the papaya from this devastating disease, nor is there now. . . .

## Genetically Engineered Crops Are Nutritious

Genetic engineering also helps achieve other goals of the organic farming movement. By reducing the use of pesticides and by reducing pests and disease, it can make farming more affordable and thus keep family farmers in business and assure local food security. It can also make food more nutritious: In 2011, plant breeders expect to release "golden rice," a genetically engineered variety that will help fight vitamin A deficiency in the developing world, a disease that contributes to the deaths of 8 million young children each year.

To successfully blend the two important strands of modern agriculture—genetic engineering and organic farming—we will need to overcome long animosity between the advocates of organic farming and conventional farmers. We also need to address the repulsion many consumers feel toward the idea of genetic engineering.

## Genetically Engineered Crops Do Not Threaten Organic Crops or Health

To many supporters of organic agriculture, genetically altering crops feels fundamentally wrong or unnatural. They believe that farmers already have enough tools for a productive and healthy farming system.

On an environmental level, many worry that genetically engineered crops will cross-pollinate nearby species to create a new kind of weed that could invade pristine ecosystems and destroy native plant populations. On a personal level, many consumers worry that genetically engineered foods are unsafe or unhealthy.

So far, however, it appears those concerns are driven more by technological anxiety than by science. Virtually all scientific panels that have studied this matter have concluded that pollen drift from genetically engineered varieties currently grown in the U.S. does not pose a risk of invasiveness. (However, this does not mean that future crop varieties will also be harmless: Each new crop variety must be considered on a case-by-case basis.) And in terms of food safety, a report by the National Academy of Sciences concluded that the process of adding genes to our food by genetic engineering is no riskier than mixing genes by conventional plant breeding.

Today 70 percent of all processed foods in the U.S. have at least one ingredient from genetically engineered corn, cotton, canola, or soybean. Unlike the well documented adverse effects of some pesticides, there has not been a single case of illness associated with these crops.

## Genetically Engineered Crops Are the Food of the Future

Pitting genetic engineering and organic farming against each other only prevents the transformative changes needed on our farms.

There seems to be a communication gap between organic and conventional farmers and between consumers and scientists. The stakes are high in closing that gap. Without good science and good farming, we cannot even begin to dream about establishing an ecologically balanced, biologically based system of farming and ensuring food security.

**EVALUATING THE AUTHOR'S ARGUMENTS:**

In this viewpoint Pamela Ronald uses facts, statistics, and examples to make her argument that genetically modified crops can alleviate world hunger. She does not, however, use any quotations to support her point. If you were to rewrite this article and insert quotations, what authorities might you quote? Where would you place the quotations, and why?

# Genetically Modified Crops Perpetuate World Hunger

**Bill Freese**

*"Commercialized GM crops are confined to soybeans, corn, cotton and canola. Soybeans and corn predominate, and are used mainly to feed animals or fuel cars in rich nations."*

Genetically modified (GM) crops do not alleviate world hunger or protect the environment, argues Bill Freese in the following viewpoint. He explains that most GM crops are used for livestock feed or biofuel materials. Freese says that in addition to the fact that these crops do not produce edible food, they take up valuable farming land, which leaves less room for food crops. Freese also suggests that GM crops produce less food than traditional crops, further contributing to the problem of world hunger. Furthermore, he asserts, they do not significantly resist disease and require more pesticide and herbicide than is usually required, which threatens the environment. Freese concludes that GM crops do not address the real causes of world hunger and in many cases contribute to the problem.

Bill Freese, "Biotech Snake Oil: A Quack Cure for Hunger," *Multinational Monitor,* September/October 2008. Copyright © 2008 by Essential Information. All rights reserved. Reproduced by permission.

Freese is a science policy analyst at the Center for Food Safety, a nonprofit group that supports sustainable agriculture and opposes genetically modified crops.

**AS YOU READ, CONSIDER THE FOLLOWING QUESTIONS:**
1. What are glyphosate-resistant weeds and how do they factor into the author's argument?
2. How do the yields of genetically modified soybean crops compare with traditional soybean crops, according to Freese?
3. Why, according to Freese, do farmers end up paying four times more for genetically modified seed than for traditional seed?

Rising global food prices reached a flash point this spring [2008], sparking food riots in over a dozen countries. Mexican tortillas have quadrupled in price; Haiti's prime minister was ousted amid rice riots; African countries were especially hard hit. According to the World Bank, global food prices have risen a shocking 83 percent over the past three years. And for the world's poor, high prices mean hunger.

The global food crisis has many causes, but according to the biotechnology industry there's a simple solution—genetically modified [GM], or biotech, crops. Biotech multinationals have been in media blitz mode ever since the food crisis first made headlines, touting miracle crops that will purportedly increase yields, tolerate droughts, grow in saline soils, and be chockfull of nutrients, to boot. . . .

Not everyone is convinced. In fact, the UN [United Nations] and World Bank recently completed an unprecedentedly broad scientific assessment of world agriculture, the International Assessment of Agricultural Knowledge, Science and Technology for Development (IAASTD), which concluded that biotech crops have very little potential to alleviate poverty and hunger. . . .

## GM Crops Feed Animals and Fuel Cars—Not People
Commercialized GM crops are confined to soybeans, corn, cotton and canola. Soybeans and corn predominate, and are used mainly to feed animals or fuel cars in rich nations. For instance, Argentina and

Soybeans, corn, cotton, and canola are the top four genetically modified (GM) crops grown around the world. Critics of GM food note that most of these are nonfood crops; yields are generally used for biofuels or livestock feed.

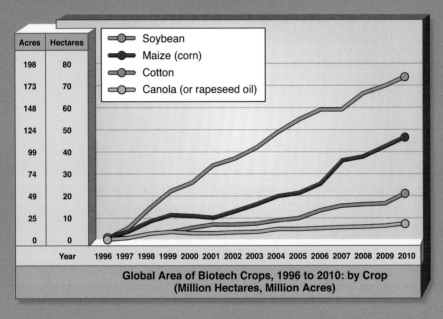

**Global Area of Biotech Crops, 1996 to 2010: by Crop (Million Hectares, Million Acres)**

Taken from: Clive James, *ISAAA Report on Global Status of Biotech/GM Crops,* ISAAA Brief 42-2010, International Service for the Acquisition of Agri-Biotech Applications, 2010.

Brazil export the great majority of their soybeans as livestock feed, mainly to Europe and Japan, while more than three fourths of the U.S. corn crop is either fed to animals or used to generate ethanol for automobiles. Expanding soybean monocultures in South America are displacing small farmers, who grow food crops for local consumption, and thus contribute to food insecurity, especially in Argentina and Paraguay. The only other commercial GM crops are papaya and squash, both grown on miniscule acreage.

Most revealing, however, is what the biotech industry has engineered these crops for. Hype and promises of future innovations notwithstanding, there is not a single commercial GM crop with increased yield, drought-tolerance, salt-tolerance, enhanced nutrition or other attractive-sounding traits touted by the industry. Disease-resistant GM crops are practically non-existent.

"We have yet to see genetically modified food that is cheaper, more nutritious or tastes better," says Hope Shand, research director for the Ontario-based ETC Group. "Biotech seeds have not been shown to be scientifically or socially useful." . . .

## GM Crops Increase Pesticide Use

According to a 2004 study by Charles Benbrook, former executive director of the Board on Agriculture of the National Academy of Sciences, herbicide-tolerant crops have also led to a substantial increase in pesticide use. Benbrook's study found that adoption of herbicide-tolerant crops in the United States increased weed-killer use by 138 million pounds from 1996 to 2004 (while insect-resistant crops reduced insecticide use by just 16 million pounds over the same period).

The vast majority of herbicide-tolerant crops are Monsanto's "Roundup Ready" varieties, tolerant to the herbicide glyphosate, which is sold under the brand-name Roundup. The dramatic rise in glyphosate use associated with Roundup Ready crops has spawned an epidemic of glyphosate-resistant weeds, just as bacteria evolve resistance to an overused antibiotic.

> **FAST FACT**
>
> A 2008 UN/World Bank–sponsored report compiled by four hundred scientists concluded that GM crops do little to solve the problems of hunger, poverty, and climate change, and that better alternatives are available.

Farmers respond to resistant weeds by upping the dose of glyphosate and by using greater quantities of other herbicides, such as the probable carcinogen 2,4-D (a component of Agent Orange) and the endocrine-disrupting weed killer atrazine, recently banned in the European Union. Glyphosate-resistant weeds and rising herbicide use are becoming serious problems in the United States, Argentina and Brazil. . . .

## GM Crops Have Low Yield

What about yield and profitability? The most widely cultivated biotech crop, Roundup Ready soybeans, actually suffers from a 5–10

*Herbicide-tolerant crops have led to a substantial increase in pesticide use. The United States increased the use of weed killer by 138 million pounds from 1996 to 2004.*

percent lower yield versus conventional varieties, according to a University of Nebraska study, due to both adverse effects of glyphosate on the soybean's nutrient uptakes, as well as unintended effects of the genetic engineering process used to create the plant. Unintended, yield-lowering effects are a serious though little-acknowledged technical obstacle of genetic engineering, and are one of several factors foiling efforts to develop viable GM crops with drought-tolerance, disease-resistance and other traits.

Monsanto says yield problems occurred only in the first year Roundup Ready soy was introduced, and that initial problems have been cured. "The first year we came out with Roundup Ready soybeans, there was a slight yield drag, but we improved the [seed] in subsequent years," says Brad Mitchell, Monsanto spokesperson.

Critics dispute this assertion, citing a 2007 study by Kansas State University which found that Roundup Ready soybean yields continue to lag behind those of conventional varieties.

## GM Crops Bankrupt Farmers

Clive James of ISAAA points to the Asian experience with GM cotton, where he says small farmers are benefiting from biotech. More than 7 million farmers—representing some of the poorest in China are seeing yields rise by 10 percent and pesticide use decline by half, he says. Farmer income is rising by approximately $220 a year, according to James.

But reviews of the Asian experience with GM cotton suggest that yield benefits are due more to good weather and other factors, not the use of biotech crops, and that GM cotton engineered for the shorter growing season in the U.S. sometimes fails to ward off targeted pests in India's longer growing season. It is true that insect resistant crops can reduce yield losses when infestation with targeted pests is severe. However, because cotton is afflicted with so many pests not killed by the built-in insecticide, biotech cotton farmers in India, China and elsewhere often apply as much chemical insecticide as growers of conventional cotton. But because they have paid up to four times as much for the biotech seed as they would for conventional seed, they often end up falling deeper into debt. Debt is an overriding problem among small farmers in developing countries, and any policies or technologies that deepen farmer debt have drastic consequences. Each year, hundreds of cotton farmers in India alone commit suicide from despair over insurmountable debts.

Even the U.S. Department of Agriculture (USDA) has found no economic benefit to farmers from growing GM crops in most situations. . . .

## We Need to Address the Real Causes of Hunger

Biotech mania has also diverted attention from the underlying social causes of the food crisis, which include diversion of food crops to make biofuels, and "trade liberalization" policies that have crippled developing country agriculture and made these nations dependent on subsidized surpluses from rich nations. "The structural causes" of the food crisis, says Anuradha Mittal, executive director of the Oakland Institute, "lie in policies of international financial institutions over the last 20 to 30 years, which have made developing countries so vulnerable in the first place." International Monetary Fund (IMF) and World Bank policies, she says, "eroded state and international investment in agriculture," as well as farmer support mechanisms such as state grain marketing agencies and subsidized agricultural services.

The IMF and World Bank also "promoted cash crops instead of domestic production of food for domestic consumption. All of those policies have basically removed the principle of self-sufficiency. At the same time, you have had the lowering of tariffs which has resulted in the dumping of cheap, subsidized commodities from rich countries. With all of those policies, you find an erosion of the agricultural base of developing countries and their ability to feed themselves," says Mittal. . . .

## GM Crops Are All Hype

The tremendous hype surrounding biotechnology has obscured some basic facts. Most GM crops feed animals or fuel cars in rich nations; are engineered for use with expensive weed killers to save labor; and are grown by larger farmers in industrial monocultures for export. "GM crops have nothing to do with feeding hungry people and nothing to do with sustainability," says Shand. "With the consolidation of the seed industry, seed companies' primary objective is to increase profits by restricting farmers' reliance on saved seeds."

> **EVALUATING THE AUTHOR'S ARGUMENTS:**
>
> Bill Freese and the author of the previous viewpoint, Pamela Ronald, come to starkly different conclusions about whether GM crops reduce or contribute to world hunger. Compare and contrast each author's arguments on the following topics: pesticides, crop yield, and engineered crops' ability to feed the planet's growing population. Lay out the position of each author on each topic, including at least one piece of supporting evidence. Then, state with which author you ultimately agree.

# Genetically Engineered Meat Is Better for the Environment than Non-engineered Meat

*"In addition to cutting feed-supplement costs, Enviropig could help farmers comply with 'zero discharge' rules in the United States that allow no nitrogen or phosphorous runoff from animal operations."*

## Anne Minard

In the following viewpoint Anne Minard reports on the development of a genetically engineered pig that produces environmentally friendly waste. Pig waste is typically loaded with phosphorous, which is toxic to land, water, and other creatures. Geneticists therefore created a pig whose DNA contains a special enzyme that helps the pig eat its food more efficiently and thus produce less of the harmful phosphorous in its waste. In addition to making the pig's waste cleaner, the genetic modification also saves farmers money on feed materials, which are usually infused with the enzyme that the

Enviropig contains in its genes. Minard reports that advances like the genetically modified pig could, if approved by the US Food and Drug Administration, make animal farming a cleaner and cheaper endeavor.

Minard is an environment and technology writer whose work has appeared in the *Arizona Daily Sun*, *New York Times*, and *National Geographic*, where this viewpoint was originally published.

**AS YOU READ, CONSIDER THE FOLLOWING QUESTIONS:**
1. How do phosphorous levels in Enviropig's urine and feces compare with those of a traditional pig, according to Minard?
2. What is a dead zone and how does it factor into the author's report?
3. In your own words, describe the process by which scientists developed the Enviropig.

M ove over, bacon. Here comes something greener.

## Engineered Animals Take Less Toll on the Environment than Non-engineered Animals

A genetically engineered pig recently approved for limited production in Canada makes urine and feces that contain up to 65 percent less phosphorous, officials have announced.

That could be good news for lakes, rivers, and ocean deltas, where phosphorous from animal waste can play a role in causing algal blooms. These outbursts of algae rapidly deplete the water's oxygen, creating vast dead zones for fish and other aquatic life.

Dubbed Enviropig, the genetically altered animal cleared a major hurdle last month [February 2010], when the government-run Environment Canada approved the animal for production in controlled research settings.

The new biotech pig could take years to pass U.S. and Canadian tests for commercial use and human consumption, noted Steven Liss, an environmental scientist at the University of Guelph in Ontario and a spokesperson for the project.

But the Enviropig's creators are hopeful the animal will eventually pass muster.

"This will be probably the most significant transgenic food to be approved. We're in new territory," Liss said.

## Solving a Dirty Problem

Like all living things, pigs need phosphorous from their food, because the element plays a key role in the formation of bones, teeth, and cell walls as well as in a variety of cellular and organ functions.

Swine in the United States primarily eat corn, while those in Canada munch on cereal grains, including barley. But the kind of

*Genetically altered pigs, which have been dubbed "Enviropigs," are able to process phosphorous more efficiently than other pigs.*

phosphorous that occurs naturally in those plants is indigestible without an enzyme called phytase, which pigs lack.

Most farmers feed their pigs this enzyme as a supplement. But ingested phytase isn't as effective at breaking down phosphorous as phytase created inside the pig would be, so a fair amount of the element gets flushed out in pig waste. That waste, in turn, can make its way into the water supply.

Enviropig would eliminate the need for added phytase, because the animal has been engineered to make its own.

## Modified Animals Are More Efficient and Cheaper than Regular Animals

Researchers spent more than a decade hunting for an enzyme in nature responsible for breaking down phosphorous, finally finding it in the genome of the bacterium *E. coli*.

### FAST FACT

Canada's University of Guelph claims its genetically engineered Enviropig eats less feed and produces less waste, including 30–65 percent less toxic phosphorous waste, than regular pigs. This is better for the environment, the school says, because it decreases the chemical contamination of farm drainage areas.

To make sure the modification would work in mammals, the team paired the *E. coli* genes with a mouse DNA promoter, a section of DNA that encourages replication of a specific segment—in this case the bacterial genes. Researchers then injected microscopic fertilized pig embryos with the mixture.

Early trials revealed that the bacterial enzyme was not only incorporated into the pig genome, it could be inherited by the genetically engineered pigs' offspring.

"We are now in the eighth generation of pigs, and it has been transmitted to all of those generations," said Cecil Forsberg, a University of Guelph microbiologist and lead researcher on the project.

"And from our testing, there is no change in the structure of the gene throughout those generations."

With the added genes, Enviropig is able to absorb more phosphorous from its feed, so less of the element ends up unused and excreted.

# Genetically Engineered Animals

The Enviropig has been genetically engineered by scientists at the University of Guelph, in Ontario, Canada. The pig has a gene for making the enzyme phytase added to its DNA. This allows it to digest plant phosphorous more efficiently than conventional pigs can.

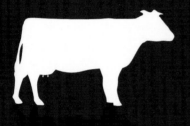

A biotech company called BioDak, LLC is working to create cows that are resistant to bovine spongiform encephalopathy, otherwise known as "mad cow disease," a disease that has crippled cow populations in certain regions and poses a threat to human health.

Researchers at the Cambridge Veterinary School and the Roslin Institute are working to produce a flock of chickens that are immune to avian flu, which has devastated chicken populations around the world.

Researchers at the University of Rhode Island have blocked a gene in rainbow trout that inhibits muscle differentiation and growth. This has produced a bigger-than-normal rainbow trout with "six-pack abs" and broad shoulders.

Taken from: The University of Guelph and Jennifer Walsch, "TastyTransgenics," *Scientist*, July 28, 2010.

Enviropig addresses not only environmental concerns but also societal challenges in pig farming, the University of Guelph researchers say.

In addition to cutting feed-supplement costs, Enviropig could help farmers comply with "zero discharge" rules in the United States that allow no nitrogen or phosphorous runoff from animal operations.

Right now, most pork producers meet this law by collecting pig waste in pits and lagoons until it can be treated or recycled as fertilizer—resulting in added expenses for the farmers.

"The cost to produce animals is increasing, putting the burden on farmers in a global marketplace," project spokesperson Liss said.

## Engineered Animals Could Be the Future

Now that Enviropig has reached a milestone, pork producers will be watching to see if the transgenic animal passes safety tests with the U.S. Food and Drug Administration [FDA], noted Paul Sundberg, vice president of science and technology for the U.S. National Pork Board.

Industry professionals will also want to see a cost-benefit analysis, to be sure Enviropig will be a boon to the industry, Sundberg said.

"Pork producers are in favor of any technologies that can increase their competitiveness," he said.

So far, no transgenic animal has been approved for consumption in the United States. But in 2008 the FDA announced approval of the first human health product made from a genetically engineered animal.

The goat-derived anticoagulant, ATryn, is used for the prevention of blood clots in patients with a rare disease-causing protein deficiency.

**EVALUATING THE AUTHOR'S ARGUMENTS:**

In this viewpoint Anne Minard reports that a genetically engineered pig's waste contains less phosphorous than a normally bred pig and is thus better for the environment. How does the Food and Water Watch, author of the following viewpoint, directly respond to this claim? List at least two points the group makes in response.

# Genetically Engineered Meat Is Not Environmentally Friendly

**Food and Water Watch**

> *"The approval of Enviropig will lead to more intense applications of manure that can lead to harmful environmental effects."*

Food and Water Watch is a nonprofit organization that advocates for technologies and policies that result in safe food and access to clean drinking water. In the following viewpoint the group argues that genetically modified animals such as the Enviropig do not offer environmental benefits, and may even hurt the environment. Food and Water Watch explains that the Enviropig was genetically modified so its waste would contain less phosphorous, which is toxic to the environment. In fact, because of phosphorous's toxicity, there are limits on how much manure can be produced by any one farm. But Food and Water Watch predicts that farmers who use Enviropigs will likely just cram more manure onto their farms until they meet maximum phosphorous requirements, rather than hosting fewer animals. It also argues that Enviropig's waste contains other toxic elements that will continue to threaten the environment. Finally, Food and Water Watch says that genetically engineered animals have not been adequately vetted for health risks posed to humans who eat them. For all of these reasons it concludes that a better solution to environmental problems posed by pig farming is to host fewer animals per farm, even though this does not yield as much profit.

**AS YOU READ, CONSIDER THE FOLLOWING QUESTIONS:**
1. Why, according to the author, will the total amount of phosphorous that ends up in land around a farm raising genetically modified pigs likely not be much lower than levels around a traditional pig farm?
2. What harmful by-products aside from phosphorous does the author say are found in pig excrement?
3. What percentage of Americans say they support the genetic modification of animals, according to the author?

Enviropig™ is the trade name for a genetically engineered hog currently being developed at the University of Guelph in Ontario, Canada. Enviropig is being marketed as an improvement in swine physiology that will lead to less water pollution. So what makes this designer pig so environmentally friendly? As it turns out, not much at all.

## The Creation of Enviropig

For proper nutrition, pigs require a certain amount of phosphorous in their diets. However, the phosphorous in standard feed grains is difficult for pigs to digest, and the phosphorous that doesn't get absorbed ends up in manure. When hogs are raised on enough land to spread their waste, there is no need for concern. In fact, phosphorous is actually a very valuable fertilizer for crops when used in appropriate amounts.

"Appropriate," however, is not the right term when talking about concentrated animal feeding operations, or CAFOs, which are often described as factory farms. In factory farms, thousands of animals are confined in a single facility and they collectively produce a tremendous amount of waste that needs to be dealt with. The pressure to dispose of this incredible amount of waste can lead to overapplication of manure on land and accidental discharges from storage pits. When the waste ends up running off into surface water or seeping into groundwater, excess phosphorous can cause algae blooms, fish kills and other environmental damage. According to the U.S. Department of Agriculture (USDA), only 20 to 50 percent of all large hog farms have enough land on which to spread all their manure without exceeding limits on phosphorous or nitrogen application. Because of its danger to humans and the environment, phosphorous is one of the major nutrients monitored in U.S. Environmental Protection Agency CAFO regulations.

So where does Enviropig fit into all of this? The genetically modified hogs produce an enzyme known as "phytase" that allows them to absorb the phosphorous from feed more efficiently, resulting in less phosphorous in the manure. Phytase was approved by the U.S. Food and Drug Administration (FDA) in 1995 and was first available to producers in 1997. But with Enviropig, researchers have genetically engineered an animal that can secrete the phytase enzyme in its own mouth, which reduces the need for phytase to be provided as a feed supplement.

**FAST FACT**

According to GM-Free Ireland's website, genetically modified soy production in South America (for European Union livestock feed) has caused the ruin of 21 million hectares of forest in Brazil, 14 million in Argentina, and 2 million in Paraguay.

So isn't Enviropig an improvement? Not really. The only setting in which Enviropig's unique new trait offers any utility is on a factory farm. The factory farm model of raising pigs is so detrimental to the environment—not to mention the health of the animals and the people who eat them—that generating slightly less phosphorous in the huge amounts of waste produced will not come close to fixing the problem.

## Enviropig Is Not Environmentally Friendly

The fact that Enviropig can reduce the level of phosphorous present in manure does not necessarily translate into a positive impact on the environment. First, the actual amount of waste that the Enviropig produces is not reduced in any meaningful way; the chemical makeup of the waste is just modified. Second, the actual amount of phosphorous that ends up in the land around the CAFO will most likely stay the same. Why? As the scientists working on Enviropig have implied, use of these modified animals simply allows CAFO facilities to apply more manure to their land before they exceed regulated limits on phosphorous. According to researchers at the University of Guelph, "The land area required for spreading [the same amount of manure] could be reduced by 33%." This means that more manure can be applied before reaching regulatory limits on other nutrients, and therefore the concentration of potentially damaging chemicals and nutrients applied to the land besides phosphorous, like excess nitrogen, could actually increase, not decrease.

## Phosphorous Is Not the Only Problem with Pig Excrement

There are many serious concerns with manure besides just phosphorous. There are issues with misapplication and overapplication of manure on land. The amount of manure produced in a large hog CAFO is actually so great that some facilities have turned to shipping out manure to other areas, which can be quite expensive.

There are other harmful and dangerous products in hog manure, including nitrogen, ammonia, and hydrogen sulfide. Nitrogen, which hogs excrete in greater quantities than phosphorous, has similar negative effects on waterways including fish kills and algae blooms, and can cause health problems in humans, including "blue-baby syndrome" in infants. Nitrogen pollution is also thought to be largely responsible for the "dead zone" in the Gulf of Mexico. Ammonia is toxic to aquatic life and reduces the amount of oxygen in water bodies, therefore reducing the ability of the water to support an ecosystem. Both ammonia and hydrogen sulfide can lead to respiratory ailments, and hydrogen sulfide can cause central nervous system effects. With the potential for Enviropig to concentrate more manure in one place, the likelihood for all of these other negative impacts increases.

## Phytase Is Already Available as an Inexpensive Feed Supplement

Phytase, the enzyme that Enviropig has been genetically modified to produce in its mouth, is already available as a feed supplement. Because of their inability to digest the phosphorous in feed grains, pigs typically need to ingest additional phosphorous in order to meet their dietary needs. So while a phytase supplement may be an added cost, producers using it don't have to pay for additional phosphorous to meet the hogs' nutritional needs, and in some cases this may make them more profitable. Furthermore, there may be a significant cost difference between regular pigs and the Enviropig. While the researchers behind Enviropig contend that it may be more efficient than the phytase supplement, even they acknowledge that any potentially increased performance of Enviropig's genes over a supplement must be considered within the context of the major cost of developing a genetically engineered animal.

*The US Department of Agriculture reports that 20 to 50 percent of all large hog farms lack sufficient land on which to spread their pigs' manure without exceeding allowable regulatory limits on phosphorous and nitrogen.*

## More Thorough Review Is Needed

Research on genetically engineering a pig that can produce phytase began over 10 years ago. Scientists first genetically engineered mice to secrete phytase in their saliva, and then used that gene to engineer pigs to do the same. In February 2010, the University of Guelph cleared the first regulatory hurdle when it received approval from the Canadian Environmental Protection Agency to reproduce the animal in confined conditions. The evaluation only considered whether the pig was actually toxic to the environment. The university has identified both the United States and China as lucrative markets for Enviropig, and the researchers have already submitted materials to the U.S. FDA and the Canadian Food Inspection Agency for approval to market the pig.

In order for Enviropig to be sold for food in the United States, it must first be approved by the FDA. The FDA does not have regulations in place on how to approve genetically engineered animals, but in 2009, the FDA issued voluntary, non-binding guidance for the industry. In the guidance, the FDA stated that it is currently using the animal drug approval process for approving genetically engineered animals. This is flawed for a number of reasons.

The animal drug approval process is not transparent. Despite the fact that the agency plans to hold public advisory committee meetings prior to approval, there is still minimal room for public participation before the agency makes a decision on a proposal. More concerning is that the FDA will be basing its conclusions on materials provided by the researchers themselves. In addition, FDA will not evaluate the claimed positive environmental impact of Enviropig or whether the genetic engineering simply duplicates a function already available in a cheap feed supplement. FDA's analysis of the animal's "effectiveness" only consists of determining whether the genetic modification is expressed in the animal.

## Americans Oppose Genetically Modified Animals

Consumers are increasingly aware of genetic manipulation in food animals and they don't like what they see. A Pew Initiative poll in 2006 found that 64 percent of adults are "uncomfortable" or "strongly uncomfortable" with animal cloning, and a 2005 poll found that only *27* percent of people surveyed supported the genetic modification of animals. The sentiment was so strong that in 2008 the USDA asked producers to voluntarily keep cloned animals off the market because of consumer concerns. Even if these products do come to market, consumers should have the opportunity to make informed choices about their food. A recent Consumers Union poll found that 95 percent of consumers favor labeling meat and milk that comes from genetically engineered animals. Yet despite this overwhelming support, the FDA will not require labeling food that comes from genetically modified animals like Enviropig.

The problem with excess phosphorous in hog waste is the result of too many animals being concentrated in too little space, not a problem of genetics. The approval of Enviropig will lead to more intense applications of manure that can lead to harmful environmental effects. Instead of addressing actual environmental harms that CAFOs pose, scientists are spending years working on a genetic modification to engineer a solution to a problem that simply would not occur if hogs were not confined with too many animals and too little land.

## EVALUATING THE AUTHOR'S ARGUMENTS:

To make its argument, Food and Water Watch presents poll statistics that show Americans are wary of eating genetically modified animals. What do you think? Would you eat pork from a pig that had been genetically engineered? What kinds of studies would you need to see performed before you were confident the meat was safe for consumption?

**Viewpoint**

**5**

# Genetically Engineered Fish Can Solve the Overfishing Crisis

**James Greenwood**

*"The AquAdvantage salmon ... could ease pressure on wild fish stocks, reduce the environmental impact of traditional fish farming, and help feed the growing world population."*

In the following viewpoint James Greenwood argues that society should embrace genetically engineered (GE) fish. He explains that GE fish are just like traditional fish, except for having minor genetic alterations that make them grow much faster. Fast-growing, laboratory-created fish are desperately needed, according to Greenwood, because wild fish stocks have been critically depleted, and the world faces a severe fish shortage. In his opinion, genetically engineering fish is the only way to ease the pressure on wild fish stocks and prevent certain fish species from going extinct. It is also the best way to prevent fisheries from going out of business and the best way to feed the many societies that rely on fish to sustain them, he says. Greenwood concludes that GE fish are healthy and safe and should be embraced as the best solution to the overfishing crisis.

James Greenwood, "Genetically Engineered Fish Is Answer to Seafood Crisis," *Natural Resource Report,* October 3, 2010. Copyright © 2010 by Biotechnology Industry Organization. All rights reserved. Reproduced by permission.

Greenwood is president and chief executive officer of the Biotechnology Industry Organization, a group that advocates for the interests of biotechnology companies.

**AS YOU READ, CONSIDER THE FOLLOWING QUESTIONS:**
1. What percentage of the world's fish stocks does Greenwood say are fully exploited or overexploited?
2. How much does it cost to ship farm-raised salmon from Chile to the United States, according to Greenwood?
3. What is an ocean pout and how does it factor into the author's argument?

Right now [in October 2010], the government is deciding whether it's safe for us to eat genetically engineered salmon. The fish, called AquAdvantage, is being developed by a Massachusetts biotech firm and is in every measurable way identical to Atlantic salmon—except it grows to normal size twice as fast. If officials at the Food and Drug Administration (FDA) give it the green light, it would be the first time that a genetically engineered animal is approved for food use.

Generic engineering usually conjures up images of Frankenstein. But modern day biotech researchers are anything but mad scientists. Their ground-breaking work has the potential to address world hunger and protect the environment. The AquAdvantage salmon in particular could ease pressure on wild fish stocks, reduce the environmental impact of traditional fish farming, and help feed the growing world population.

## Genetically Engineered Salmon Could Save the Fishing Industry

Overfishing and pollution are quickly wiping out the native global fish supply. Already 80% of fish stocks world-wide are fully exploited or overexploited, according to a May 2010 U.N. [United Nations] report. If current trends continue, virtually all fisheries risk running out of commercially viable catches by 2050.

*According to the author, wild fish populations are quickly diminishing, and fish farms, like this one in Alaska, can help solve the problem.*

Fish farming has helped address this problem: About half of seafood consumed world-wide is now farm-raised. But it's expensive. Shipping farm-raised salmon to the United States from Chile, where most of our fish originates, costs as much as 75 cents per pound.

Faster-growing genetically engineered salmon could help restore America's domestic fish farming industry, trimming costs and reducing energy consumption. If the FDA approves the fish it would also spur investment in other food products. This could help meet the world's growing demand for protein-rich food.

## Genetically Engineered Fish Pose No Threat to Wild Fish Stocks

Through biotechnology, scientists at a firm in South Dakota have developed cattle that are resistant to mad cow disease. Canadian researchers have asked the FDA to approve their "Enviropig," a pig genetically engineered to produce manure that is less polluting. Biotech researchers are also exploring ways to fortify food plants with enhanced nutritional content, which could help alleviate malnutrition and certain diseases in the developing world. And researchers are engineering animals that can better utilize nutrients in feed.

Critics contend that genetically engineered fish haven't been sufficiently researched and could harm our health. But the truth is that these faster-growing salmon are the result of more than two decades of research. Plus, the FDA's system to ensure the safety of such animals has been in development for over a decade.

There's nothing peculiar about this fish's genetic makeup. To create the faster-growing salmon, scientists took a gene from the Chinook salmon, which matures rapidly, along with a gene from a salmon relative called ocean pout, which produces growth hormones all year. Aside from these two tweaks, the AquAdvantage salmon is chemically and biologically identical to the salmon we purchase at the local grocer.

Critics also fear that these salmon could crossbreed with wild fish and pollute their gene pool. This is highly unlikely given the protections put in place and the realities of the science. By treating the genetically engineered eggs, all AquAdvantage salmon will develop as sterile females. And these fish will be grown in contained, land-based tanks, away from any interaction with wild fish and the ocean.

> **FAST FACT**
>
> According to the Food and Drug Administration, genetically engineered (GE) salmon that have been injected with a growth hormone gene require 10 percent less feed than non-injected fish, which would make the GE fish plentiful and cheaper to produce.

## Genetically Engineered Food Is Healthy and Safe

When genetically engineered crops were introduced 14 years ago, critics worried that "frankenfood" would hurt human health and the environment. Since then, farmers have grown corn, soybeans, cotton and other products that are resistant to disease and pests, and

Genetically engineered (GE) salmon grow faster and reach maturity earlier than standard salmon; in fact, they reach market size twice as fast as traditional salmon. This could help fish farmers save money and make it cheaper to raise fish in inland pens, reducing the need for ocean pens. Since the GE salmon are sterile, proponents of this practice say they cannot threaten wild populations.

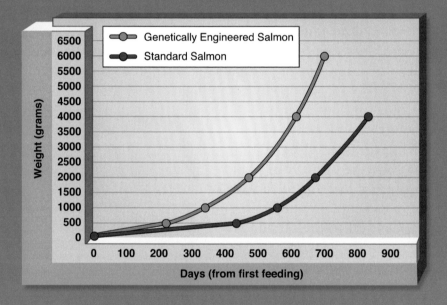

Taken from: AquaBounty Technologies, 2011. www.aquabounty.com/products/products-295.aspx.

tolerant of herbicides. These innovations have reduced production costs, increased agricultural productivity and reduced agriculture's footprint on the environment. To date, not a single adverse health effect has been caused by a food derived from genetically engineered crops.

Genetically engineered animals are the next intelligent step in food innovation. As Josh Ozersky, a James Beard Award–winning food writer, has observed, "There are no Black Angus cows grazing in the wild; they're the product of breeding for size, marbling and fast growth, not unlike the genetically-modified salmon."

Public dialogue on any new technology is important. But the discourse must be based on sound science. And regarding faster-growing salmon—and other genetically engineered foods of the future—science shows clearly that they can provide us with the safe and sustainable food source we need.

## EVALUATING THE AUTHOR'S ARGUMENTS:

James Greenwood represents the Biotechnology Industry Organization, a group that advocates for the interests of biotechnology companies. The author of the following viewpoint, the Yukon River Drainage Fisheries Association, represents the interests of salmon fisheries in Alaska. Does knowing the background of these two authors influence your opinion of their arguments? Are you more inclined to trust one over the other? Why or why not?

# Genetically Engineered Fish Threaten Wild Fish Populations

## Yukon River Drainage Fisheries Association

*"The threats of a GE salmon to wild salmon populations are substantial . . . [including] pollution, disease, food competition and genetic contamination."*

The Yukon River Drainage Fisheries Association (YRDFA) represents the interests of salmon fishers along the Yukon River in Alaska. In the following viewpoint they argue that genetically engineered (GE) fish should not receive approval from the Food and Drug Administration (FDA) because they threaten wild fish populations. According to the YRDFA, GE fish will likely escape from their pens and mate with wild fish, spreading disease to the wild fish and competing with them for food. If this happens, wild populations would likely die out in just a handful of generations. In addition to the threat to wild fish, the YRDFA warns that GE fish pose a threat to humans: The association says GE fish are less nutritious than wild fish and may contain allergens and even cancer-causing

Becca Robbins Gisclair, Yukon River Drainage Fisheries Association, Letter to Division of Docket Management, Regarding Docket No. FDA-2010-N-0385—Labeling of AquAdvantage Genetically Engineered Salmon, November 22, 2010.

hormones. For all of these reasons YRDFA urges the FDA to prevent GE fish from being marketed in the United States.

**AS YOU READ, CONSIDER THE FOLLOWING QUESTIONS:**
1. What is the "Trojan gene" effect and how does it factor into the author's argument?
2. How many pounds of wild fish does it take to grow one pound of farmed salmon? How does this factor into the author's argument about GE salmon?
3. How does the vitamin and mineral content of GE salmon compare with that of wild salmon, according to the author?

Thank you for the opportunity to comment on the approval and labeling of the AquAdvantage genetically engineered salmon. YRDFA is an association of commercial and subsistence fishers on the Yukon River, Alaska's longest river. The region we represent is home to some of the world's most prolific salmon resources, and the world's furthest migrating salmon runs on the Yukon River. These salmon provide a primary source of food and are essential to the continued viability of the subsistence way of life in Western Alaska. For many residents the commercial salmon harvest also provides the only means of income for those who live in the remote villages of the Yukon River.

As amplified below, we strongly oppose the approval of the genetically engineered (GE) salmon and urge the FDA [Food and Drug Administration] to reject GE salmon. Should the FDA decide to approve the AquAdvantage GE salmon despite overwhelming opposition, clear, mandatory labeling must be required for all product types under all circumstances.

## GE Fish Pose Serious Risks to Wild Fish Populations

The threats of a GE salmon to wild salmon populations are substantial, as the threats from salmon farms—including pollution, disease, food competition and genetic contamination—are compounded with the farming of a GE salmon which grows twice as fast. Millions of farmed salmon have escaped from open-water net pens, outcompeting wild populations for resources and straining ecosystems. We believe any approval of GE salmon would represent a serious threat to the survival of native wild salmon populations, many of which have already suffered severe declines.

Escape of GE farmed salmon into the wild carries the risk that genetic material from these fish will invade the wild gene pools of native Pacific salmon populations. Nature is rife with examples of such genetic introgression and such gene pool mixing is common among fish, and members of family Salmonidae are no exception. Indeed, [researchers have] documented that the largest members of the Pacific salmon (Chinook salmon) are capable of successful reproduction in the wild with the smallest members of their genus (pink salmon). The fact that both species were introduced to the environment where the genetic introgression occurred (the Laurentian Great Lakes) and that pink salmon were introduced accidentally when eggs from an "isolated" hatchery were disposed of is particularly chilling in the context of concerns about the AquaBounty [developer of AquAdvantage salmon] proposal to contain GE salmon eggs.

Research on such genetic pollution resulting from what scientists call the "Trojan gene" effect published in the *Proceedings of the National Academy of Sciences* notes that a release of just sixty GE fish into a wild population of 60,000 would lead to the extinction of the wild population in less than 40 fish generations.

## The Final Blow to Fish Stocks

If the FDA approves the AquAdvantage salmon, GE fish will likely be among the millions of salmon that currently escape from open ocean pens every year. This could be the final blow to wild salmon stocks, and in turn the thousands of men and women who depend on fishing for their livelihoods.

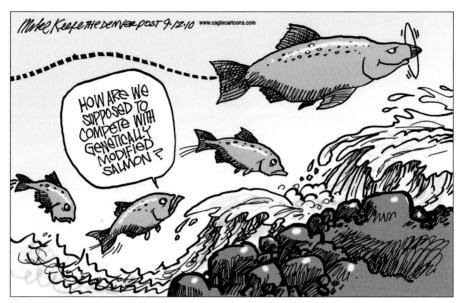

© 2010 Keefe, *The Denver Post,* and PoliticalCartoons.com.

Even if grown in contained, land-based facilities, the "farming" of fish is already harming salmon fishermen. In addition to the threat of these GE salmon displacing native salmon populations, such fish farming encourages the propagation of deadly fish diseases, the concentration of harmful wastes and industrial drugs and chemicals escaping into open waters, and the over-fishing of vast quantities of non-commercial fish to feed carnivorous farmed fish, such as salmon. It generally takes three pounds of wild fish to grow one pound of farmed salmon. Since the AquAdvantage salmon have been engineered for fast growth, it stands to reason that their feed requirements will be even higher. Wild Atlantic salmon are already on the Endangered Species List in the U.S.; approving these GE Atlantic salmon will undoubtedly add to the burden on wild stocks.

## GE Fish Pose Serious Risks to Human Health

There is substantial concern that the routine use of antibiotics to control diseases often found in farmed fish may impact human health. Transgenic [genetically modified] fish may be susceptible to more diseases than fish currently grown in aquaculture facilities because transgenic fish are identified as "macro-mutants" with a reduced ability to survive. Consequently, the amount of antibiotics given to transgenic fish may be higher than the amount currently given to farmed fish; already farmed salmon are given more antibiotics than any other livestock by weight.

In addition, for both growth hormone and another insulin-like hormone, IGF-1, there are no data on levels in the flesh of triploid

*Ocean-caught King salmon sit on ice at a Seattle fish market. Many people are concerned that genetically modified salmon may pose a health risk.*

GE salmon, because only inappropriate and insensitive tests were used to try and detect it. Given this lack of data on two of the identified potential hazards of this GE fish, rather than state that there are no problems, FDA should say that this study is of insufficient quality and needs to be redone using more sensitive test methods. In addition, prior to this GE salmon being approved, the company should provide data on the levels of growth hormone and IGF-1 in the muscle of triploid GE salmon that have been raised in Panama, not at the PEI facility [on Prince Edward Island, Canada, where the GE salmon eggs in question were produced]. This is particularly important for IGF-1, a hormone linked to a number of cancers. GE salmon also may be more allergenic than non-GE salmon.

## If Approved, GE Fish Must Be Labeled

GE salmon has several differences which qualify as "material" and therefore mandate required labeling. One of these differences is changes in the composition of salmon from the insert of the AquAdvantage genetic construct. The vitamin and mineral content of GE salmon is also worse than in other farmed salmon. The AquAdvantage salmon may be more allergenic than other salmon and contains less healthy fatty acids than do other farmed salmon.

If approved, clear, mandatory labeling for GE fish must be required for all product types under all circumstances to protect U.S. salmon markets. Many salmon caught and processed in the United States are sold in foreign markets. If GE fish are not labeled, there will be confusion over which U.S. salmon products are GE and which are not. This could significantly impact markets for all salmon fishermen. Labeling would allow those nations and consumers who wish not to buy genetically engineered products a clear choice in the market place.

## GE Fish Should Not Receive FDA Approval

In closing, the AquAdvantage GE salmon should not be approved because of the risks to wild salmon and human health, and we urge the FDA to not approve this product. Should the FDA decide to approve the AquAdvantage GE salmon despite overwhelming opposition, clear, mandatory labeling must be required for all product types under all circumstances.

The Yukon River Drainage Fisheries Association warns that GE fish will mate with wild fish and genetically contaminate that population. How does James Greenwood, author of the previous viewpoint, directly respond to this claim? Do you think what Greenwood suggests will solve the problem of cross-genetic contamination? Why or why not? Quote from both texts in your answer.

# Chapter 3

# How Should Genetic Engineering Be Regulated?

*A researcher analyzes genetically modified spruce sprouts. Many questions remain about the safety of genetic engineering.*

# Genetic Engineering Needs to Be Heavily Regulated

*Scientific American*

The following editorial was originally published in *Scientific American*. The author argues that genetic engineering needs to be heavily regulated to make sure it remains ethical and safe. The author describes a cutting-edge medical technique that allows parents to test embryos for genetic diseases before they are implanted in the womb. Although this technique has prevented thousands of babies from being born with crippling genetic diseases, the author warns it could be used for more superficial purposes, such as to design a baby with specific cosmetic traits or superior qualities. The author laments that at present, no official federal regulations exist to guide the many ethical questions raised by this very serious prospect. Doctors who profit from the procedure should not be trusted to regulate their use of it, and laws need to be ready for

> **"The intricacies of regulating fertility technology requires more careful consideration that can only come with a measure of federal guidance."**

the slew of questionable cases that are likely on the horizon. *Scientific American* concludes that the United States must create a federal regulatory body that will oversee the fast-growing and ethically sensitive world of genetic engineering.

**AS YOU READ, CONSIDER THE FOLLOWING QUESTIONS:**
1. Who is Nadya Suleman and how does she factor into the author's argument?
2. How much might a physician receive to perform preimplantation genetic diagnosis (PGD)? What problem does the author see with this?
3. What rules has the United Kingdom's Human Fertilization and Embryology Authority come up with for in vitro fertilization and embryo manipulation? List at least three.

O n March 3 the cover story of the *New York Daily News* trumpeted a simple imperative to "Design Your Baby." The screaming headline related to a service that would try to allow parents to choose their baby's hair, eye and skin color. A day later the Fertility Institutes reconsidered. The organization made an "internal, self regulatory decision" to scrap the project because of "public perception" and the "apparent negative societal impacts involved," it noted in a statement.

The change of heart will do nothing to stymie the dawning era of what the article called "Build-A-Bear" babies. The use (and abuse) of advanced fertility technology that evokes fears of *Gattaca, Brave New World* and, of course, the Nazis' quest for a blonde, blue-eyed race of Aryans continues apace. A recent survey found that about 10 percent of a group who went for genetic counseling in New York City expressed interest in screening for tall stature and that some 13 percent said they would be willing to test for superior intelligence. The Fertility Institutes is still building the foundation for a nascent dial-a-trait catalogue: it routinely accepts clients who wish to select the sex of their child.

The decision to scrap the designer baby service came just a few weeks after Nadya Suleman, a single, unemployed California mother living on food stamps, gained notoriety after giving birth to octuplets through in vitro fertilization. The Suleman brouhaha showed that even routine uses of reproductive technologies can be fraught with issues that bear on ethics and patient safety.

The preimplantation genetic diagnosis (PGD) technique used by the Fertility Institutes to test embryos before implantation in the womb has enabled thousands of parents to avoid passing on serious genetic diseases to their offspring. Yet fertility specialists are doing more than tiptoeing into a new era in which medical necessity is not the only impetus for seeking help. In the U.S., no binding rules deter a private clinic from offering a menu of traits or from implanting a woman with a collection of embryos. Physicians who may receive more than $10,000 for a procedure serve as the sole arbiters of a series of thorny ethical, safety and social welfare questions. The 33-year-old

*Nadya Suleman, the "Octomom," is seen at an in vitro clinic in Los Angeles. She gave birth to octuplets through in vitro fertilization, and her pregnancy raised questions about the ethics and safety of reproductive technology.*

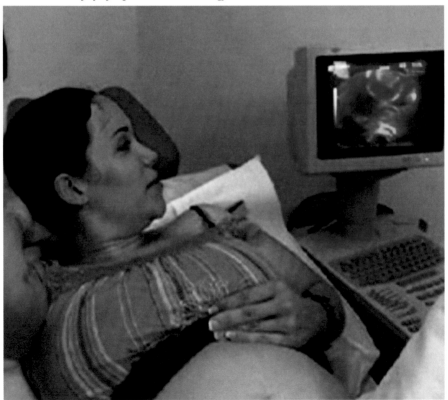

Suleman already had six children, and her physician implanted her with six embryos, two of which split into twins. American Society for Reproductive Medicine (ASRM) voluntary guidelines suggest that, under normal circumstances, no more than two embryos be transferred to a woman younger than 35 because of the risk of complications.

Of course, any office consultation with a fertility doctor will likely neglect the nuances of more encompassing ethical dilemmas. Should parents be allowed to pick embryos for specific tissue types so that their new baby can serve as a donor for an ailing sibling? For that matter, should a deaf parent who embraces his or her condition be permitted to select an embryo apt to produce a child unable to hear? Finally, will selection of traits perceived to be desirable end up diminishing variability within the gene pool, the raw material of natural selection?

**FAST FACT**

A 2010 Gallup poll found that 75 percent of Americans would vote for laws to increase government regulation of food safety.

In the wake of the octuplets' birth, some legislators made hasty bids to enact regulation at the state level—and one bill was drafted with the help of antiabortion advocates. The intricacies of regulating fertility technology requires more careful consideration that can only come with a measure of federal guidance. As part of the push toward health care reform, the Obama administration should carefully inspect the British model.

Since 1991 the U.K.'s Human Fertilization and Embryology Authority (HFEA) has made rules for in vitro fertilization and any type of embryo manipulation. The HFEA licenses clinics and regulates research: it limits the number of embryos implanted and prohibits sex selection for nonmedical reasons, but it is not always overly restrictive. It did not object to using PGD to pick an embryo that led to the birth of a girl in January who lacked the genes that would have predisposed her to breast cancer later in life.

# How Disease-Free Babies Are Selected

In 2009 British scientists successfully "designed" a breast cancer–free baby using the steps described below. The process is controversial for several reasons. Many embryos were discarded in the search for one with cancer-free DNA, and some consider this similar to murder. Others worry that trait-selecting will move from preventing diseases to more cosmetic preferences, such as eye or hair color.

1. **A man inherits a gene which has caused breast cancer in three generations of his family.**

2. **His wife takes drugs to boost egg production, and the couple undergo IVF to create up to 15 embryos.**

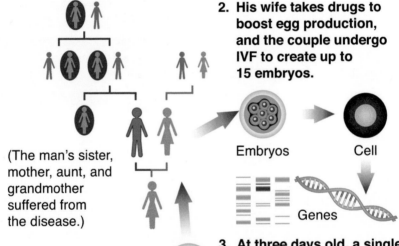

(The man's sister, mother, aunt, and grandmother suffered from the disease.)

Embryos     Cell

Genes

3. **At three days old, a single cell is taken from each embryo. The DNA is extracted and tested using chemicals which will show up in the defective gene. Six embryos were found to have the breast cancer gene and were discarded.**

4. **Two of the healthy embryos are transferred into the woman, who becomes pregnant with a cancer-free baby.**

Taken from: Sam Greenhill, Jenny Hope, and Nick McDermott, "Britain's First Cancer-Free Designer Baby Born After Being Screened for Deadly Gene," *Daily Mail* (London), January 11, 2009.

HFEA may not serve as a precise template for a U.S. regulatory body. But a close look at nearly two decades of licensing a set of reproductive technologies by the country that brought us the first test-tube baby may build a better framework than reliance on the good faith of physicians who confront an inherent conflict of interest.

**EVALUATING THE AUTHOR'S ARGUMENTS:**

In this viewpoint the author uses facts, examples, and reasoning to make the argument that genetic engineering needs to be regulated by the federal government. The viewpoint does not, however, use any quotations to support this point. If you were to rewrite this article and insert quotations, what authorities might you quote? Where would you place the quotations, and why?

**Viewpoint**

**2**

*"Drawing so much attention to such outlandish propositions [as designer babies] simply distracts attention from . . . efforts that could materially benefit the poor, powerless and dispossessed today."*

# Genetic Engineering Is Not Yet Enough of a Reality to Warrant Heavy Regulation

**Andy Coghlan**

In the following viewpoint Andy Coghlan argues there is no pressing need to regulate the creation of genetically designed babies. In his opinion, such a scenario is not likely to become reality for a long time, if ever. Coghlan thinks it is unreasonable for people to fear a world in which parents will choose their baby's eye color, height, or design their intelligence, and even less reasonable to fear a world that is divided into a superclass of genetically modified people and an underclass of traditional people. He explains that most experiments involving genetic engineering have aimed to improve human health or reduce disease. No one has sought to create a so-called "designer baby," as many have feared. Moreover, given the intricacies of the science and the catastrophic consequences of genes gone wrong, Coghlan thinks it is unlikely that people will even be interested in such a prospect. He concludes that rather than stressing over the need to regulate what has not yet happened, society should seek to address the political, social, and economic inequalities that hurt people today.

Coghlan is a senior reporter for *New Scientist*, which originally published this article.

**AS YOU READ, CONSIDER THE FOLLOWING QUESTIONS:**
1. Who is David King and how does he factor into the author's argument?
2. What does Coghlan find "laughable" about the fear that a race of super-intelligent babies might be genetically engineered?
3. What is a greater contributor to two-tiered societies than the prospect of genetically engineered people, according to Coghlan?

Has a GM [genetically modified] master race been created? Well, not quite. There is a way to go yet before blonde-haired, blue-eyed Aryan clones genetically engineered with hyper intelligence are frog-marching into the White House, the Kremlin [Russia's center of government] and the United Nations to take over the world and condemn the rest of us inferiors to perpetual slavery.

## The Doom-Mongers Need to Relax
And yet, according to doom-mongers, the first goose-step towards a master race has apparently been taken through creation of a "GM human embryo".

"It will very soon be used to create 'enhanced designer babies'," says David King of Human Genetics Alert [HGA], the UK lobbying group which issued a press release on 11 May [2008] publicising the "breakthrough".

"This would turn children into objects, designed just like other consumer commodities, and would lead to a new eugenics in which the rich are able to give their children genetic advantages over others," says King, whose organisation timed its publicity to coincide with a forthcoming vote by the UK parliament on new legislation which could legalise modification of human embryos for research purposes.

"When I discovered these experiments on the internet, I was shocked at these scientists' irresponsibility," says King. "This might seem like a small thing, but it is a large first step on the road that will likely lead to the nightmare world of designer babies and a new eugenics. We may be entering the era of human genetic modification, which would be no less significant for humanity than the nuclear era," says the press release from HGA.

Now, let's get down to finding out the truth of this latest peril visited on the human race.

### Experiments Have Targeted Disease

First, it turns out that the experiment was done and reported last September [2007] at a meeting of the American Society of Reproductive Medicine. A team led by Nikica Zaninovic of the Weill Medical College of Cornell University in New York used a harmless lentivirus to ferry, into human and mouse embryos, genes that make green or red fluorescent proteins, substances that glow green or red when exposed to ultraviolet light. The same genes are added to cells routinely to enable researchers to visually track engineered cells.

The engineered cells reached the blastocyst stage of about 100 cells, and were destroyed at five days. The mouse embryos survived a bit longer and yielded colonies of mouse embryonic stem cells which also glowed green or red, proving that the stem cells carried the same genetic alteration as the embryos.

"The genetic engineers gave him that birthmark as part of a sponsorship deal."

"The genetic engineers gave him that birthmark as part of a sponsorship deal," cartoon by RGJ - Richard Jolley. www.CartoonStock.com.

So what possible uses could this have if it worked in human embryos? Quite a few, it turns out. By obtaining and growing genetically modified stem cells from diseased embryos, for example, it might be possible to track and understand genetic changes that would lead to disease in adult humans, providing new targets for possible treatments.

Equally, by adding, subtracting or disrupting genes, it should be possible to identify genes vital for healthy embryos to develop, and enable screening during fertility treatment for embryos doomed from the outset. Alternatively, genes might be added to improve the chances of obtaining viable embryonic stem cells from human embryos. Because embryonic stem cells grow into every tissue in the body, this could provide new ways of growing tissue outside the body for transplant into patients.

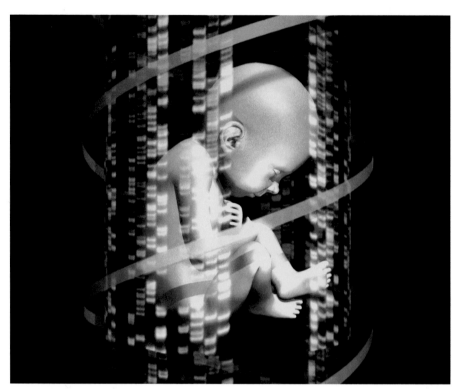

*Scientists say that genetically engineering human babies is too dangerous to consider, since such procedures are irreversible.*

## More Fiction than Fact

No one is contemplating King's "nightmare" scenario: the creation of genetically-engineered babies. The aim is simply to provide new avenues of research on disease and infertility. It may not work, or create any useful information. But if we don't try, how can we know?

And even if it was legal to create GM babies, the idea of implanting them with genes that make them super-intelligent geniuses is laughable. Recent studies have shown that human intelligence is dependent on a huge number of genes, with even the most significant individual genes contributing no more than a minuscule fraction of a percent to someone's brainpower.

More importantly, as scientists themselves have recognised, genetic engineering of human babies is too dangerous to contemplate because such changes, whether in embryos, sperm or eggs, would be irreversible in a recipient and inherited by all the baby's descendants. If the change malfunctioned, this would be catastrophic. As we know from gene therapy experiments to correct inherited mutations that cause immune deficiencies, the process can activate genes that lead to cancer. So as well as being technically imperfect, inherently unsafe, genetically worthless and illegal, such processes are doomed to failure even if they were affordable by the "super rich".

King rightly rues the inequalities that throughout history have led to discord in society. But as far as two-tier societies are concerned, it would make more sense to focus on correcting the social, political and economic inequalities that are here and now, and have been for millennia. Throughout history, money, influence and nepotism have been used unashamedly to give children a leg-up over their peers.

## Designer Babies Are a Long Way Off

It's a fair bet that marrying someone intelligent, handsome or athletic is far more likely than genetic tinkering to give someone ambitious the "designer" child they want. Perhaps making political and economic systems fairer in the here-and-now would do more to narrow the gap between rich and poor than a ban on a hypothetical technology which has zero chance of widening the existing divide between rich and poor.

If anything, drawing so much attention to such outlandish propositions simply distracts attention from political and economic efforts that could materially benefit the poor, powerless and dispossessed today. Let's get that sorted. Then we can start worrying about things that are pure science fiction.

## EVALUATING THE AUTHOR'S ARGUMENTS:

Andy Coghlan's argument hinges on the assumption that it is unlikely that designer babies will become a reality any time soon. Do you think the authors of the following two viewpoints in this chapter would agree with him? Why or why not? Write one or two sentences about each author, summing up their positions on this issue. Then state your thoughts on the matter.

**Viewpoint**
**3**

# Laws Should Prevent Parents from Selecting Genetically Imperfect Children

### Daniel Finkelstein

*"Parents [should be prohibited] from screening the embryos and then perversely ensuring that their child cannot hear. I am afraid that making such a choice is child abuse."*

Parents should not be able to choose to have a disabled child, argues Daniel Finkelstein in the following viewpoint. He discusses a case in which deaf British parents, who are undergoing fertility treatments, want the right to select an embryo that is also deaf. Finkelstein understands that all parents want their children to reflect their best traits, but rejects the parents' view that deafness should count as an enviable trait. Finkelstein thinks it is unconscionable to purposefully impose a disability on one's child. Parents should seek the best for their children, and ensuring a disability is not in any child's best interest, he says. Finkelstein concludes that parents should not have the right to select for disabilities when they undergo fertility treatment.

Finkelstein is a weekly columnist for the London newspaper the *Times*. He also posts his opinions at his blog, *Comment Central*.

## AS YOU READ, CONSIDER THE FOLLOWING QUESTIONS:

1. What does Finkelstein say is the difference between serious long-term physical disability and temporary inability? How does this factor into his argument?
2. Regarding genetic engineering, what amounts to child abuse, in the author's opinion?
3. What does the British Human Fertilisation and Embryology Act say must be done with embryos that are significantly at risk of having a serious disability, according to Finkelstein?

The poet/comedian John Hegley hates people who wear contact lenses. He thinks they are traitors. Glasses, he says, are "a symbolic celebration of the wider imperfection that is the human condition". Contact lenses are "a betrayal of humanity".

Don't laugh. There is probably someone out there who takes him seriously and thinks he's right.

On Monday morning the *Today* programme featured a deaf activist by the name of Tomato Lichy. Mr Lichy opposes a new law that will forbid people undergoing IVF [in vitro fertilization] from deliberately choosing a deaf child. Why? Because he believes that deafness is not a disability.

## A Terribly Wrong Proposal

He said he felt sorry for hearing people. In a deaf club "you would be the one with the disability", he told [host] John Humphrys, "because you can't use sign language". He said that he and his deaf wife actively hoped that their child would be deaf and were pleased when it turned out she was.

And listening to him I thought—this man is immensely articulate, immensely courageous and immensely, terribly, wrong.

I don't want you to think, however, that he is immensely alone. At the end of the interview, Mr Lichy claimed that his position on deafness and disability was the official stance of many of the big mainstream organisations for deaf people. And you know what? On that, he's right.

Just to take one example, the mission statement of the Royal Association for Deaf People (patron, the Queen; president, the Archbishop of Canterbury) states: "Deaf people are only 'disabled' by the effects of discrimination and exclusion." Meanwhile, the British Deaf Association and the Royal National Institute for Deaf and Hard of Hearing People strongly support the right of deaf people deliberately to select a deaf child.

So why would big, well-meaning organisations adopt such an extreme position? One that, if they could persuade the rest of us to accept it, would lead to poor defenceless babies coming into the world purposefully made deaf by their parents. It is because of three separate serious pieces of muddled thinking.

## We Cannot Let People Choose Disability

The first one was right there in Mr Lichy's interview—he has confused a serious long-term physical disability with a temporary inability. Mr Humphrys can learn sign language, should he wish, while Mr Lichy cannot, sadly, learn hearing.

The second is a confusion about the new law. The Human Fertility and Embryology Bill going through Parliament[1] contains a clause that says that embryos with a significant risk of serious disability "must not be preferred to those that are not known to have such an abnormality".

Deaf campaigners say that this is eugenics. Wrong. The aim is to prevent eugenics, a warped eugenics that deliberately selects deafness.

---

1. The bill became law in November 2008.

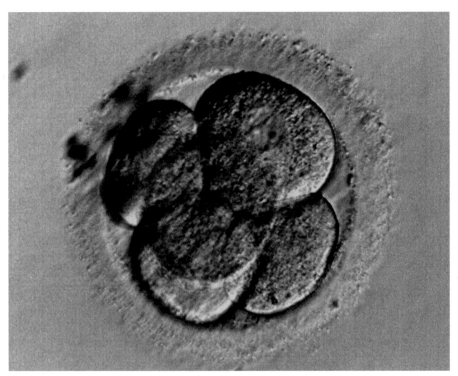

*A five-cell human embryo is pictured two-and-a-half days after conception. The British Human Fertility and Embryology Bill states that embryos with a substantial risk of serious disability must not be selected over healthy embryos.*

The law forbids parents with a political or cultural agenda from screening the embryos and then perversely ensuring that their child cannot hear. I am afraid that making such a choice is child abuse.

The biggest confusion, however, is the third one—their muddled thinking about equality. They are confused between the idea of being equal and being treated equally.

## The Truth About Equality

The mission statement of the Royal Association for Deaf People asserts that: "Deaf and Hearing people are equal and should receive the same levels of opportunity, access and respect." The second half of this sentence is obviously right. Of course deaf and hearing people should receive the same levels of opportunity, access and respect—none of these things should vary with your ability to hear.

But what does the first part of the sentence, the idea that deaf and hearing people are equal, even mean? That deaf and hearing people are exactly the same? Obviously they aren't. Take two deaf people and they won't be equal to each other let alone to someone else. We are all different.

This confusion is a very common one. The idea is that in order to protect the ideas of equal respect and equality under the law we must believe that every human being is born the same and that differences between them are entirely created by the environment, and the way we humans relate to each other.

The alternative view—we are all born different from each other in personality as well as physical attributes and that genes account for a great deal of the variability of our behaviour—is regarded with a mixture of fear, revulsion and denial. When I dared to raise this in a political discussion recently, one person called me Dr [Josef] Mengele[2] while others looked at me as if I had gone mad.

In his magnificent book *The Blank Slate*, the Harvard professor Steven Pinker, untangles this mess. That we are the product of our nature and not just the environment is now, scientifically, beyond question. Our genetic make-up heavily influences who we turn out to be.

## It Is Wrong to Purposefully Impose Disabilities on Children

Is this an argument for eugenics? Of course not. To start with, there is nothing to say that such engineering is possible, anyway. [Nobel Prize–winner] George Wald put it brilliantly when he was asked to donate to a bank of sperm from Nobel scientists: "You should be contacting people like my father, a poor immigrant tailor. What have my sperm given the world? Two guitarists!" But even if it were possible, that wouldn't make it right. As Tomato Lichy suggests, people might want to select some pretty odd characteristics.

Is it an argument for racism? Of course not. Even supposing anybody could convincingly show systematic racial differences in an attribute like intelligence, which they have not, this would not justify treating somebody as a category rather than as a person.

Is it an argument for discriminating against the disabled? Of course not. In fact, the opposite. And that is what the deaf campaigners don't

2. A Nazi doctor who conducted horrible experiments on people he considered undesirable.

appear to understand. It is precisely because deafness is, of course it is, a disability, that equality of treatment is difficult to guarantee and has to be fought for so hard.

I said Mr Lichy was courageous. It is courageous to refuse to lie down and be a victim. I can only admire that. But it is one thing to be strong, almost heroic, about his own misfortune, quite another to want it imposed upon a child.

**EVALUATING THE AUTHOR'S ARGUMENTS:**

Daniel Finkelstein argues that deafness is a disability that should not be preferred to hearing. Dominic Lawson, the author of the following viewpoint, likens deafness to an identity trait with its own culture, such as a religion or an ethnicity. From his perspective, it is reasonable for parents to want to pass on their culture to their children; Finkelstein disagrees. After reading both viewpoints, what is your position on this issue? Should parents be allowed to willingly pass on a disability to their children? Why or why not?

# Laws Should Allow Parents to Select Genetically Imperfect Children

**Dominic Lawson**

"*Being deaf is a positive thing, with many wonderful aspects. . . . We don't see members of [other] minority groups wanting to eliminate themselves.*"

In the following viewpoint Dominic Lawson argues that laws should not prevent parents undergoing fertility treatments from choosing to have a disabled child. He discusses a case in which British parents, who are deaf, want the right to select an embryo of theirs that is also deaf. Lawson argues that deafness is like a cultural trait in that it informs how a family communicates with each other, experiences the world, what they value, find funny, or meaningful. In his view, it is reasonable for deaf parents to want to share this with their child. Lawson is not bothered by the fact that "normal" embryos created in the fertility treatment process would be discarded in favor of a deaf one: The reality of such treatments require healthy embryos to be discarded all the time, he says. Lawson concludes it is reasonable for parents not to view their disability as negative and to want their child to share in their culture and their lifestyle.

Lawson is a reporter for the London-based newspaper the *Independent.*

**AS YOU READ, CONSIDER THE FOLLOWING QUESTIONS:**
  1. What is "cultural deafness" and how does it factor into the author's argument?
  2. What can a person not be said to miss, according to Lawson?
  3. Why might a child specifically chosen for his deafness not be upset with his parents, according to the author?

Few broadcasters convey astonishment with an undertone of outrage as skilfully as the BBC's John Humphrys. Over the years the *Today* programme presenter has had a lot of practice. Yesterday [March 10, 2008], however, it was not an equivocating politician who got Humphrys to hit his top note. It was a bloke called Tomato—Mr Tomato Lichy, to be precise. The programme's listeners never actually heard Mr Lichy speak: he responded to John Humphrys' questions in sign language, and someone else turned his answers into spoken English for the interviewer's—and our—benefit.

Tomato Lichy and his partner Paula are both deaf. They have a deaf child, Molly. Now Paula is in her 40s and the couple believe they might require IVF [in vitro fertilization] treatment to produce a second child. They very much want such a child also to be deaf.

## Do Not Discriminate Against People with Disabilities

Here's where it gets political: the Government is whipping through a new Human Fertilisation and Embryology Bill. Clause 14/4/9 states that, "Persons or embryos that are known to have a gene, chromosome or mitochondrion abnormality involving a significant risk that a person with the abnormality will have or develop a serious physical or mental disability, a serious illness or any other serious medical condition must not be preferred to those that are not known to have such an abnormality."[1]

1. The bill became law in November 2008.

This, Tomato Lichy signed to Mr Humphrys, means that he and his partner would be compelled by law to discard the very embryos that they wished to have implanted: "I couldn't participate in any procedure which forced me to reject a deaf embryo in favour of a hearing embryo." Mr Lichy argued that this legislation was specifically designed to discriminate against deafness. As a matter of fact, he's quite right.

The explanatory notes to the clause inform legislators: "Outside the UK, the positive selection of deaf donors in order deliberately to result in a deaf child has been reported. This provision would prevent (embryo) selection for a similar purpose." This all stems from a single case in the US six years ago, when a lesbian couple, Sharon Duchesneau and Candace McCullough, both of whom were deaf, selected a sperm donor on the basis of his family history of deafness. It caused outrage—outrage which clearly filtered through to the British Health ministry.

The most revealing account of this most unusual conception appeared in an email interview in the *Lancet*. Duchesneau and McCullough wrote: "Most of the ethical issues that have been raised in regard to our story centre on the idea that being deaf is a negative thing. From there, people surmise that it is unethical to want to create deaf children, who are, in their view, disabled."

## Disabled Parents View Their Difference as Cultural

"Our view, on the other hand [McCullough goes on], is that being deaf is a positive thing, with many wonderful aspects. We don't view being deaf along the same lines as being blind or mentally retarded; we see it as paralleling being Jewish or black. We don't see members of those minority groups wanting to eliminate themselves."

This is as clear an exposition as you will see of the concept of "cultural deafness". Adherents of this philosophy refer not just to "deaf

*Some deaf parents view their condition more as a cultural circumstance than as a disability and enjoy sharing "deaf culture" with their children.*

culture"—Mr Lichy said he felt "sorry for" John Humphrys for not being able to appreciate "deaf plays"—but to themselves as members of a "linguistic community". This idea of a separate language enables the proponents of cultural deafness to describe themselves as, in effect, an ethnic minority—and thus any legislative attempt to weed them out as embryos to be analogous with the most insidious racism.

Another deaf British couple, whose child is also deaf, told the BBC's disability magazine that "it is important that our culture is passed on from one generation to another . . . the threat of losing our culture would be devastating because we have so much to show and to give."

## Do Not Presume Everyone Wants to Be "Normal"

In the most obvious sense, the argument that deafness is not a disability is self-evidently wrong. The absence of one of our most valuable senses brings with it many disadvantages on a purely practical level. So many careers are all but closed to the deaf—a deaf boy might well have fantasies about being a soldier or a fireman, but fantasies are what they will remain. Humphrys tasked Tomato Lichy with the fact that he would never be able to enjoy the music of Beethoven—a low blow, this, as Beethoven himself was vilely tormented by increasing deafness, which also put an end to his ability to conduct his own music.

Yet I don't share Humphrys's apparent incredulity at his interviewee's dismissal of the joys of music. If you have never been able to hear music, then you can not be said to miss it, or suffer from its absence from your life. Indeed, I know one or two people who are completely tone deaf, who are not in the least miserable about it: their only irritation is in occasionally having to hear what to them is just undifferentiated noise, when they would rather have silence. The idea that congenitally deaf people are "suffering" in some intrinsic sense, strikes me as mere presumption.

## Deaf Parents Just Want a Similar Child

Moreover, it is not as if the implantation of an embryo which is thought likely to be deaf—and science at the moment would be very hard pushed to forecast such an outcome with any reliability at all—is equivalent to deliberate mutilation. What we are talking about is an already existing potential person; the choice isn't whether that embryo could be "made deaf" or not. The choice is whether to discard that already existing embryo for another one believed to be less at risk of turning out to be deaf.

Given that the fertilisation process within IVF generates many more test-tube embryos than are selected for implantation, there are always going to be vast quantities of 'normal' embryos which will be destroyed.

The real issue here, as Mr Lichy observed, is whether the state should be able to dictate to him and his partner which of their embryos they should be allowed to select, and which they should be compelled to reject. I am not surprised—still less, incredulous—that he can't understand why he and his partner should be prevented by law from choosing the embryo which might most turn out to resemble them.

## Existence Is More Important than Perfection

John Humphrys argued that most people would regard his demands as profoundly selfish: Mr Lichy and his partner might want a deaf child, but what about the views of the child itself? I suspect that the child in question would be intelligent enough to be able to understand that the only alternative deal for him or her was never to have existed at all.

Nevertheless, if Clause 14 of the HFE Bill does pass into law, I do hope that Mr Lichy and his partner will find it in them to love and cherish a child who is not deaf. We hearing people are not so useless, when you get to know us properly.

**EVALUATING THE AUTHOR'S ARGUMENTS:**

Dominic Lawson and Daniel Finkelstein, the author of the previous viewpoint, debate whether parents like Tomato and Paula Lichy should be allowed to purposefully have a deaf child. Imagine that you are this child. How would you feel if you knew your parents chose to let you be born disabled—in fact, selected you because of the disability? Would you be angry with them? Would you be grateful to them? Reflect on how you would feel if you were the child in this scenario. Quote from the texts you have read in your answers.

# Genetically Engineered Foods Should Be Labeled as Such

## Michael Hansen

"We feel that the process of genetic engineering constitutes a 'material fact' and, thus, that fact must be on the label."

In the following viewpoint Michael Hansen argues that genetically engineered (GE) meat and fish products should be labeled as such. He explains that the Food and Drug Administration requires labeling for any food that has two or more ingredients. In his opinion, genes that have been added to an animal count as an ingredient. Hansen also thinks that labeling is necessary because the safety of GE food is not yet proven. He warns that GE salmon might cause an allergic reaction in some people, but without labels, people will not be able to tell different kinds of salmon apart. Labeling would also help consumers decide whether they want to risk eating a food that might be nutritionally different from the natural version of a food, which GE food may be. For all of these reasons, Hansen argues that GE meat and fish should be labeled as such.

Hansen is a senior staff scientist with the Consumers Union, a nonprofit independent organization that works to ensure products are fairly marketed and safe.

**AS YOU READ, CONSIDER THE FOLLOWING QUESTIONS:**
1. What percentage of people surveyed by the Consumers Union said they thought food from GE animals should be labeled?
2. What does the phrase "act of man" mean in the context of the viewpoint?
3. What does Hansen say might not become apparent until a large population uses a product?

Consumers Union (CU) welcomes the opportunity to comment on labeling of food derived from AquAdvantage Salmon, a salmon genetically engineered with a growth hormone to reach mature size more quickly.

We disagree with both FDA's [Food and Drug Administration's] assertion that genetic engineering itself does not, in and of itself, constitute a "material" difference under the law and also with their definition of what constitutes a "material" difference. In a Consumers Union nationwide poll, 95 percent of respondents said they thought food from genetically engineered animals should be labeled, and 78 percent strongly agreed with this.

There are two legal rationales for requiring labeling of genetically engineered salmon: Genetic engineering constitutes a "material fact;" and the NAD (New Animal Drug, e.g. the genetic construct with the Chinook growth hormone gene) and/or its expression product constitutes a food ingredient. Thus, for the reasons articulated below, we feel that the process of genetic engineering constitutes a "material fact" and, thus, that fact must be on the label. . . .

## Genes Should Count as Ingredients

The ingredients labeling provision of the Food Drug and Cosmetic Act requires that any food made from two or more ingredients must have a label with the common or usual name of each ingredient. The law defines an ingredient broadly as all "those substances that have

*The author argues that because the safety of genetically modified foods has not been conclusively established, such products should be labeled.*

been used to manufacture a food." Included in this definition would be all added substances. Added substances are all those substances present in food with the exception of those that are an "inherent natural constituent" but not intrinsically part of the food. Since there is some grey area here, a federal court has ruled that the law distinguishes between substances that are present in the food due to "acts of man" and those present due to "acts of nature;" the former are considered added and therefore subject to labeling while the latter are not. This distinction is important because the law requires a higher safety standard for substances present by reason of "acts of man." As the court pointed out, "[I]f a coffee processor subjects coffee to a process in which the naturally occurring caffeine is removed and later replaced with an equal amount of identical caffeine, it seems clear that Congress would have the stricter health standard apply".

Given this logic, we feel all genetic material moved into an animal via genetic engineering techniques, and any expression products from the genes, should be considered added and, therefore, treated as an ingredient. Take the AquAdvantage salmon that is engineered to increase growth rate, for example. The genetic construct inserted in the AquAdvantage Salmon consists of a Chinook growth hormone gene, a promoter sequence from the ocean pout and a small stretch of the PUC plasmid. This genetic construct was added by an "act of man," as the gene does not . . . exist in nature. Obviously, the process whereby these different genetic materials were spliced together to form a single stretch of DNA was an act of man. Even though some might argue that the Chinook growth hormone is "natural," the process by which it is added to the Atlantic salmon renders it an "act of man" in the same way that the caffeine artificially added to a coffee bean is considered added, while the naturally occurring caffeine is not.

In our view, the added genetic material, as well as the expression products, should be considered as ingredients. In a commonsensical consumer understanding of the word ingredient, something that contains genetic material from at least two dissimilar sources contains at least two ingredients. By "dissimilar sources" we mean simply sources such as Chinook salmon, ocean pout, and *E. coli*, that have a breeding barrier between them that is not already breached by traditional breeding.

## Labeling Protects Against Uncertainty

We also believe that FDA should require labeling for food derived from GE animals as a risk management measure to deal with scientific uncertainty and to track any potential unexpected adverse health effects associated with consumption of GE animals. This would be consistent with the recommendations developed by the Codex Alimentarius Ad Hoc Intergovernmental Task Force on Foods Derived from Modern Biotechnology and adopted by the Codex Alimentarius Commission in 2003. The *Principles for the Risk Analysis of Foods Derived from Modern Biotechnology* clearly state that labeling can be used as a risk management option to deal with scientific uncertainties associated with the risk assessment of GE foods: "Risk managers should take into account the uncertainties in the risk assessment and implement appropriate measures to manage these uncertainties. Risk management measures may include, as appropriate, food labeling, conditions for market approval and post-market monitoring".

Significant scientific uncertainty exists in the risk analysis of foods derived from GE/GM, and this is recognized in the Codex. In fact, the *Guideline for the Conduct of Food Safety Assessment of Foods Derived from Recombinant-DNA Animals* has a whole section on unintended effects which clearly states that they can have an unintended effect on human health: *"Unintended effects due to genetic modification may be subdivided into two groups: those that are "predictable" and those that are "unexpected" . . . A variety of data and information are necessary to assess unintended effects because no individual test can detect all possible unintended effects or identify, with certainty, those relevant to human health."* Italics added. Furthermore, this section recognizes that the unintended effects could also be caused by changes in genes that are expressed at the molecular level and how the gene products are processed: "Molecular biological and biochemical techniques (that) can also be used to analyse potential changes at the level of gene transcription and message translation that could lead to unintended effects".

## Health and Nutritional Effects Are Unclear

It is clear from the summary FDA has presented for the AquaAdvantage genetically engineered salmon that at present there is significant uncertainty as to its possibly increased potential to cause allergic reactions, and also data suggesting that its nutritional profile is different in terms of omega-3 and omega-6 fatty acids, something very important to health. We strongly urge FDA to insist on more data on these topics before it allows this salmon on the market and to reject this product if it has increased potential for causing allergic reactions or shows adverse nutritional changes, since it would not meet the safety criteria for approval of a New Animal Drug. However, it is essential to require labeling of these salmon to be able to detect unexpected or unintended effects where FDA may not even have requested safety data. If the genetically engineered salmon caused an unexpected aller-

## Americans Want Genetically Modified Food to Be Labeled

A poll conducted by CBS News and the *New York Times* found that the overwhelming majority of Americans think foods that contain genetically modified ingredients should be labeled as such.

**"Do you think foods that contain genetically modified ingredients should be labeled as such, or don't you think this is necessary?"**

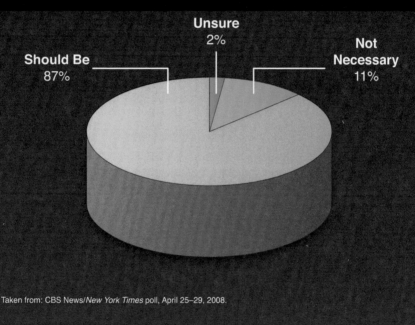

Should Be
87%

Unsure
2%

Not
Necessary
11%

Taken from: CBS News/*New York Times* poll, April 25–29, 2008.

gic reaction, or other adverse health effect, a consumer would have no way of linking their reaction to the salmon if it were not labeled, and FDA would have no way of learning of it. A consumer might eat conventional farmed salmon one week, and have no reaction, and eat the engineered salmon the next week and have a reaction, but would never attribute the reaction to the engineered salmon because it would carry no special label, and would appear to be just like the conventional salmon that the consumer had eaten without incident many times before. Thus adverse effects would occur but never be recorded, while unnecessary illnesses and possibly even deaths might be occurring.

In this regard we also urge FDA to consider the history of certain medications that were approved based on clinical trials but when widely used by consumers turned out to have caused hundred of thousands of heart attacks. It is clear that an adverse effect may not show up until a drug is used by a large population. In order to be able to track unexpected effects with genetically engineered salmon, we strongly urge FDA to require labeling as a post marketing risk management measure, as recommended by Codex guidelines.

For the reasons articulated above, FDA should require the labeling of AquAdvantage salmon and all genetically engineered animals.

## EVALUATING THE AUTHOR'S ARGUMENTS:

Michael Hansen and the *Washington Post* (the author of the following viewpoint) disagree on whether genetic material should count as a food ingredient. What do you think? Should genes count as ingredients? Why or why not? List at least two pieces of evidence that swayed you, and quote from at least one of the texts in your answer.

# There Is No Need to Label Genetically Engineered Foods

*"Demands that the altered fish be required to carry a government label seem to be more an attempt to scare off consumers than an effort to provide necessary health or nutritional information."*

*The Washington Post*

In the following viewpoint editors at the *Washington Post* say it is not necessary to label genetically engineered (GE) food. They claim that genetically altered food like salmon has been proven to be safe, nutritious, environmentally sound, and not significantly different from its natural counterpart. Forcing GE fish manufacturers to label their product, therefore, puts them at an unfair disadvantage in the marketplace, claim the *Post* editors: It gives the impression that there is something wrong with their product, which will scare off customers. The *Post* editors conclude that food labeling should be based on the safety and nutrition of a product and not the process by which it was created.

AS YOU READ, CONSIDER THE FOLLOWING QUESTIONS:
  1. What does the phrase "materially significant" mean in the context of the viewpoint?
  2. What kind of milk do the authors point out requires no label? How does this factor into their argument?
  3. What kind of labeling do the *Washington Post* editors suggest salmon sellers engage in?

I f a genetically engineered salmon is cleared for America's super-markets, it will be because of convincing evidence the fish is safe to eat and not harmful to the environment. Scientific review to date shows the fish to be indistinguishable from its traditional counterpart. So demands that the altered fish be required to carry a government label seem to be more an attempt to scare off consumers than an effort to provide necessary health or nutritional information. Clearly, there must be caution in approving the first genetically altered animal for human consumption, but government regulators should stick to their long-held, sensible rules about what information must be disclosed for the public good.

**FAST FACT**

A 2008 International Food Information Council study states that 60 percent of Americans support the Food and Drug Administration's labeling policy, which does not require GE labeling unless an allergen is introduced or the nutritional content of the food is substantially changed.

## Genetically Engineered Food Is Not Significantly Different from Other Food

The Food and Drug Administration [FDA] is considering whether to approve a fast-growing salmon developed over the past two decades by a biotech company from Massachusetts. The AquAdvantage salmon has been modified to include a gene from the Chinook salmon and DNA from an eel-like fish so that it grows twice as fast as conventional salmon. The FDA recently concluded two days of public hearings, and the expectation—based on data showing that the salmon pose no risks to humans or the environment—is that it's just a matter of time before the fish will be marketed. What has emerged as the hotbutton issue, as *The [Washington] Post*'s Lyndsey Layton reported, is labeling and the implications of that for other genetically engineered animal products likely to follow.

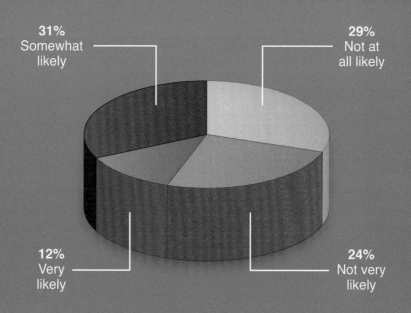

## Labels Would Deter Consumers

Americans would be less likely to buy food that was labeled as genetically modified. One poll found that 53 percent of Americans would be either not likely or not very likely to buy food that is labeled genetically modified; 43 percent would be more likely, but wary. Some say this is proof that labeling genetically modified food would deter customers.

**Question:**
**"How likely is it that you would buy food that is labeled as having been genetically modified?"**

31%
Somewhat
likely

29%
Not at
all likely

12%
Very
likely

24%
Not very
likely

Taken from: CBS News/*New York Times* poll, April 25–29, 2008.

A number of consumer groups pushing for mandatory labeling say that people have a right to know if the food they are eating comes from products that have been genetically modified. The not-so-subtle suggestion, of course, is that there is something different—or even wrong—with genetically modified food products, despite the science

## Genetically Engineerd Fish Is Nutritionally Similar to Natural Fish

In 2010 the Food and Drug Administration looked at how the genetically engineered (GE) AquAdvantage Salmon compared nutritionally to two types of non-GE fish. They found that all levels of vitamins in the GE fish (except for B6) were statistically similar to the non-GM fish. Further examination of the GE salmon's B6 levels revealed no health hazard. Overall, the Food and Drug Administration concluded the GE Salmon was nutritionally comparable to the natural fish. Proponents argue this is why special labeling for the fish would be unnecessary.

| Vitamin | Kind of Fish | Minimum Value | Maximum Value |
|---|---|---|---|
| Folic Acid | Non-GE farmed fish | 0.15 | 0.58 |
| | Non-GE control fish | 0.13 | 0.5 |
| | GE salmon | 0.09 | 0.41 |
| Niacin | Non-GE farmed fish | 80.7 | 96.4 |
| | Non-GE control fish | 63.5 | 100 |
| | GE salmon | 80.7 | 118 |
| Pantothenic acid | Non-GE farmed fish | 5.75 | 21.6 |
| | Non-GE control fish | 9.09 | 17.1 |
| | GE salmon | 6.89 | 14.8 |
| Vitamin B1 | Non-GE farmed fish | 0.05 | 0.1 |
| | Non-GE control fish | 0.06 | 0.11 |
| | GE salmon | 0.04 | 0.09 |
| Vitamin B12 | Non-GE farmed fish | 0.02 | 0.05 |
| | Non-GE control fish | 0.02 | 0.04 |
| | GE salmon | 0.01 | 0.04 |
| Vitamin B2 | Non-GE farmed fish | 0.86 | 1.2 |
| | Non-GE control fish | 0.83 | 1.49 |
| | GE salmon | 0.9 | 1.28 |
| Vitamin B6 | Non-GE farmed fish | 5.76 | 7.67 |
| | Non-GE control fish | 4.86 | 8.72 |
| | GE salmon | 6.5 | 10.21 |
| Vitamin C | Non-GE farmed fish | 1.6 | 4.6 |
| | Non-GE control fish | 1.8 | 7.5 |
| | GE salmon | 1.6 | 4.6 |

Taken from: US Food and Drug Administration, *Briefing Packet: AquAdvantage Salmon*, September 20, 2010, p.89.

*The author points out that the the US Food and Drug Administration has long permitted genetically modified (GM) crops to be sold in markets—without bearing GM labels.*

showing otherwise. The FDA's own rules say that once it is determined that a genetically modified food is not "materially significant" from naturally derived products, there is no reason to label it differently. Products from genetically modified crops, long permitted, do not carry special labels, nor does milk from cows given a growth hormone to produce more milk.

## Labels Based on Fact, Not Fear

The food labeling rules, which have been tested in the courts, are properly focused on safety and nutrition and not on aspects of production such as, say, whether the product is the result of artificial insemination or cross breeding. Voluntary labeling is allowed as long as it is not false or misleading, so producers of conventionally raised salmon can publicize that fact as long as they do so truthfully. Public comment is still being accepted by FDA officials, who say that they will study the record before issuing a ruling. They are right to be careful and to base their decision on proven facts, not unfounded fears.

## EVALUATING THE AUTHOR'S ARGUMENTS:

The *Washington Post* and Michael Hansen, the author of the previous viewpoint, disagree on whether it is appropriate to require GE foods to be labeled as such. What do you think? Do you think consumers have the right to know if they are buying GE products? Or do you think that forcing products to bear such labels puts them at an unfair and unnecessary disadvantage in the marketplace? Explain your reasoning and describe the kind of label, if any, you would like to see on the food you buy.

# Glossary

**bioethics:** The ethics of medical and biological research. Ethicists typically approach research with two questions in mind: "What is the good or right thing to do?" and "What are our obligations to one another?"

**biofuel:** Fuel made from biological raw components such as wood, soybean, or corn, as opposed to fossil fuels. Used to power vehicles and machines.

**Bt:** An insecticide made from a genetically altered bacterium (*Bacillus thuringiensis*) used to control crop pests.

**cord blood:** Blood obtained from the human umbilical cord at birth; a source of stem cells.

**dead zone:** An area of the ocean that kills or drives off fish and other sea life because it has been depleted of oxygen, usually due to pollution.

**designer baby:** A baby whose genetic makeup has been artificially selected, or "designed," by genetic engineering and combined with in vitro fertilization (IVF) to produce particular genes or characteristics.

**embryo:** A developing unhatched or unborn offspring. Also, an unborn human, especially during the first eight weeks after conception, after implantation in the uterus but before all the organs are developed.

**eugenics:** The science or biosocial theory that humans can influence evolution through selective breeding or genetic engineering.

**gene:** A unit of heredity made of a sequence of DNA that is transferred from a parent to offspring and determines the offspring's characteristics.

**genetic engineering (GE) or genetic modification (GM):** The science of manipulating the genes of an organism to produce a given protein, organism, or food that has certain traits. The first big GE success was a genetically modified bacterium that produced insulin. In crops, genes are adjusted to develop certain qualities, such as higher nutrition, less need for water, and resistance to pests, drought, cold, and flooding.

**in vitro fertilization (IVF):** A fertility technique in which multiple embryos are created outside of a woman's body and then implanted in the uterus. In this process, egg cells are fertilized by sperm outside the womb, *in vitro*. IVF is a major treatment for infertility when other assisted-reproduction methods have failed.

**organic farming:** A biological farming method that minimizes the use of chemicals while aiming to produce crops with high nutritional value and to improve long-term farmland sustainability. Also, a philosophy of farming that values resource efficiency, ecological harmony, and empathetic animal husbandry practices.

**preimplantation genetic diagnosis (PGD):** A technique where an embryo is created by in vitro fertilization and tested for gene imbalances and genetic diseases that might later cause problems for the child. This procedure may lead to the selection of only healthy babies or to the creation of a savior sibling, born to treat a sick sibling. Hypothetically, it might also be possible to select for certain traits, such as a baby's gender or eye color.

**savior sibling:** A child who is selected to genetically match and help save a sick brother or sister. The closest DNA match among the parents' fertilized embryos is selected to grow and be born as the savior sibling, while other embryos are destroyed.

**select:** To determine whether a characteristic or organism will or should survive.

**Trojan gene effect:** The theory that genetically engineered "super fish" might intentionally or accidentally be introduced into the wild. A GE fish could mate and contaminate a native population with disease or its growth gene.

**zero discharge technology:** Any industrial process designed to prevent release of harmful or toxic materials, such as phosphorous or nitrogen, into the environment.

# Facts About Genetic Engineering

## Facts About the Genetic Engineering of Human Beings

According to the Human Genome Project:

- As of 2009, the Food and Drug Administration (FDA) had not yet approved any human gene therapy product for sale.
- Current gene therapy is experimental and has not proven very successful in clinical trials.
- Gene therapy is complicated by its short-lived nature; the response of the subject's immune system; problems with "viral vectors," the viruses that carry genes into subjects; and the fact that many diseases and disorders exist on multiple genes or are the result of combined effects of genes.

As reported by the Associated Press:

- Preimplantation genetic diagnosis (PGD) can cost fifteen thousand dollars per screening.
- Of 190 clinics surveyed, 137 have provided embryo screening.
- Four clinics surveyed, or three percent, said they have helped parents use PGD to select their children to have a disability like deafness or dwarfism.
- The vast majority of clinics polled said they would not do so and thought it was unethical to design for a disability.

## Facts About Genetically Engineered Crops

According to the US Department of Agriculture (USDA) and the International Services for the Acquisition of Agri-Biotech Applications, in 2009:

- 77 percent of all soybean crops worldwide were genetically engineered.
- 49 percent of all cotton crops worldwide were genetically engineered.
- 26 percent of all corn crops worldwide were genetically engineered.
- 21 percent of all canola crops worldwide were genetically engineered.

- 95 percent of all US sugar beet crops were genetically engineered.
- 91 percent of all US soybean crops were genetically engineered.
- 88 percent of all US cotton crops were genetically engineered.
- 85 percent of all US corn crops were genetically engineered.
- 85 percent of all US canola crops were genetically engineered.

According to Physicians and Scientists for Responsible Application of Science and Technology, the most common genetically engineered foods are corn, soybeans, wheat, canola, tomatoes, potatoes, rice, cantaloupe, sugar beets, radicchio, flax, papaya, squash, oilseed rape, and alfalfa.

According to the Monsanto Company, a leader in genetically modified seeds and crops:
- A bioengineered food is thoroughly evaluated by three government organizations: the USDA must be convinced that the plant is safe to grow; the Environmental Protection Agency (EPA) determines potential environmental impacts; and the FDA evaluates risks related to eating GM foods.
- Monsanto claims it spends more than $2 million a day in research to identify, test, develop, and bring to market innovative new seeds and technologies that benefit farmers.

A US National Research Council study published in 2009 found that no adverse health effects can be attributed to genetic engineering, even though American corn consumption rose from 12.9 pounds per person annually in 1980 to 33 pounds annually by 2008. (During the same period, the production of genetically engineered corn rose from zero to 80 percent).

### Facts About Genetically Modified Animals
In a 2010 study, members of the FDA's Veterinary Medicine Advisory Committee found that the food safety tests for genetically engineered salmon should have included more data. They denied AquaBounty Technologies' application for production and sales of their AquAdvantage salmon pending this request.

According to the magazine *The Scientist*:

- Aquaculture researchers at the University of Rhode Island have produced rainbow trout with "six-pack abs" and hulk-like shoulders by blocking the gene that inhibits muscle growth and differentiation.
- BioDak, LLC produces cows that are resistant to bovine spongiform encephalopathy (mad cow disease), as well as cows that do not produce antibodies, for research purposes.
- The Cambridge Veterinary School and the Roslin Institute are creating chickens that are immune to the avian flu virus to decrease the deadly impact of the virus on chicken stocks.
- AquaBounty is using growth-hormone technology on salmon, tilapia, shrimp, and other seafood.
- Harvard Medical School scientists are inserting a gene into pigs that will allow them to convert the omega-6 fats found in their normal feed into omega-3s, a healthier fat.

## Facts About Food Labeling

The Non-GMO Project states that 400 US and Canadian retailers, including Whole Foods, Seeds of Change, and Nature's Way, now support a campaign to display a recognizable "Non-GMO" seal for consumers to identify non-GM foods.

The nonprofit Institute for Responsible Technology offers a free iPhone app called *ShopNoGMO* that consumers can access to identify non-GM brand choices across twenty-two grocery categories.

According to a 2008 International Food Information Council poll covering how Americans feel about current FDA biotech labeling:

- 33 percent strongly support the FDA's labeling.
- 27 percent somewhat support it.
- 27 percent are neutral.
- 8 percent somewhat oppose it.
- 5 percent strongly oppose it.
- 14 percent of consumers would like to see more information on food labels.

According to a 2008 *Consumer Reports* National Research Center survey, American consumers want the USDA label "naturally raised" to refer to meat that comes from an animal that
- had a diet free of chemicals, drugs, and animal by-products (86 percent want this);
- was raised in a natural environment (85 percent want this);
- ate a natural diet (85 percent want this);
- was not cloned or genetically engineered (78 percent want this);
- had access to the outdoors (77 percent want this);
- was treated humanely (76 percent want this); and
- was not confined (68 percent want this).

## Americans' Opinions of Genetic Engineering
According to the Pew Research Center:
- 72 percent of Americans polled say human genetics research does more good than harm.
- 19 percent feel it does more harm than good.

According to a 2006 poll conducted by the British publication *The Spectator:*
- 52 percent of Britons think that parents should not be able to pick and choose their child's traits for any reason.
- 42 percent said they should be able to pick and choose their child's traits in some cases.
- 2 percent said they should be able to in all cases.
- 4 percent said they were unsure.

Data collected by the Genetics & Public Policy Center has revealed the following about American opinions and knowledge about genetic testing:
- 97 percent of Americans have heard of cloning.
- 90 percent have heard of in vitro fertilization.
- 89 percent have heard of genetic testing.
- 83 percent have heard of prenatal testing.
- 48 percent have heard of genetic modification.
- 40 percent have heard of preimplantation genetic diagnosis (PGD).
- 67.6 percent approve of using PGD to identify fatal diseases.
- 39.9 percent approve of using PGD to select for gender.
- 27.9 percent approve of using PGD to select for non-disease traits.

According to a 2008 CBS News/*New York Times* poll:

- 17 percent of Americans have heard or read a lot about foods that contain genetically modified ingredients.
- 39 percent of Americans have heard or read some about foods that contain genetically modified ingredients.
- 27 percent of Americans have not heard or read much about foods that contain genetically modified ingredients.
- 17 percent of Americans said they have heard or read nothing about foods that contain genetically modified ingredients.
- 87 percent of Americans think that foods that contain genetically modified ingredients should be labeled as such.
- 11 percent of Americans think that foods that contain genetically modified ingredients should not be labeled as such.
- 2 percent were unsure.
- 12 percent said they would be very likely to buy food that is labeled genetically modified.
- 31 percent said they would be somewhat likely to buy food that is labeled genetically modified.
- 24 percent said they would be not very likely to buy food that is labeled genetically modified.
- 29 percent said they would be not at all likely to buy food that is labeled genetically modified.
- 4 percent were unsure.

# Organizations to Contact

The editors have compiled the following list of organizations concerned with the issues debated in this book. The descriptions are derived from materials provided by the organizations. All have publications or information available for interested readers. The list was compiled on the date of publication of the present volume; the information provided here may change. Be aware that many organizations take several weeks or longer to respond to inquiries, so allow as much time as possible for the receipt of requested materials.

**Alliance for Bio-Integrity**
2040 Pearl Ln., Ste. 2, Fairfield, IA 52556
(206) 888-4852
e-mail: info@biointegrity.org • website: www.biointegrity.org
The Alliance for Bio-Integrity is a nonprofit group that opposes the use of genetic engineering in agriculture and works to educate the public about the dangers of genetically modified foods. Position papers argue against genetic engineering from legal, religious, and scientific perspectives, including "Why Concerns About Health Risks of Genetically Engineered Food Are Scientifically Justified."

**American Life League (ALL)**
PO Box 1350, Stafford, VA 22555
(540) 659-4171 • fax: (540) 659-2586
e-mail: info@all.org • website: www.all.org
ALL is a Catholic pro-life organization that opposes abortion, artificial contraception, reproductive technologies, and fetal experimentation. It asserts that it is immoral to perform experiments on living human embryos and fetuses, whether inside or outside of the mother's womb. The league's publications include the brochures *Stem Cell Research: The Science of Human Sacrifice* and *Human Cloning: The Science of Deception.*

**Biotechnology Industry Organization (BIO)**
1201 Maryland Ave. SW, #900, Washington, DC 20024
(202) 962-9200 • fax: (202) 488-6301
e-mail: info@bio.org • website: www.bio.org

BIO represents biotechnology companies, academic institutions, state biotechnology centers, and related organizations that support the use of biotechnology in improving health care, agriculture, efforts to clean up the environment, and other fields. The organization publishes fact sheets on issues related to genetic engineering, including "Facts and Fiction About Plant and Animal Biotechnology."

**Center for Bioethics & Human Dignity (CBHD)**
2065 Half Day Rd., Deerfield, IL 60015
(847) 317-8180
e-mail: info@cbhd.org • website: www.cbhd.org

The CBHD is an international education center whose purpose is to bring Christian perspectives to bear on contemporary bioethical challenges. Its publications address genetic technologies with titles such as "Biotechnology's Brave New World." The center has initiated projects such as Do No Harm: The Coalition of Americans for Research Ethics.

**Center for Food Safety (CFS)**
660 Pennsylvania Ave. SE, #302, Washington, DC 20003
(202) 547-9359 • fax: (202) 547-9429
e-mail: office@centerforfoodsafety.org
website: www.centerforfoodsafety.org

The CFS is a nonprofit public interest organization working to protect human health and the environment by challenging harmful food production technologies and promoting organic and sustainable alternatives. It offers legal, scientific, and grassroots support to citizens and organizations concerned with food safety and sustainable agriculture. The CFS produces a quarterly newsletter *Food Safety Now!* and provides in-depth analysis of food safety topics in *Food Safety Review.*

**Center for Genetics and Society**
1936 University Ave., Ste. 350, Berkeley, CA 94704
(510) 625-0819 • fax: (510) 665-8760

e-mail: info@geneticsandsociety.org
website: www.geneticsandsociety.org

The Center for Genetics and Society is a nonprofit organization that advocates for the responsible use of genetic technology in the areas of health care, human reproduction, and agriculture. It favors a cautious approach, including bans on the use of some genetic technologies that it deems threatening to public safety and human rights. Its website contains informational and editorial articles on human genetic engineering as well as the results of numerous public opinion polls on the topic.

## Council for Biotechnology Information
1201 Maryland Ave. SW, Ste. 900, Washington, DC 20024
(202) 962-9200
e-mail: cbi@whybiotech.com • website: http://whybiotech.com

The Council for Biotechnology Information is composed of biotechnology companies and trade associations promoting the benefits of biotechnology in agriculture, industry, science, and health care. Its website offers numerous reports and FAQs on subjects such as the economic and environmental impact of genetically engineered crops.

## Council for Responsible Genetics (CRG)
5 Upland Rd., Ste. 3, Cambridge, MA 02140
(617) 868-0870 • fax: (617) 491-5344
e-mail: crg@gene-watch.org • website: www.gene-watch.org

The CRG is a national nonprofit organization of scientists, public health advocates, and others who promote a comprehensive public interest agenda for biotechnology. Its members work to raise public awareness about genetic discrimination, patenting life forms, food safety, and environmental quality. CRG publishes *GeneWatch* magazine.

## Family Research Council (FRC)
801 G St. NW, Washington, DC 20001
(202) 393-2100 • fax: (202) 393-2134
website: www.frc.org

The FRC is a Christian think tank and lobbying organization that promotes the traditional family unit based on Judeo-Christian values. It advocates for national policies that protect the sanctity of human life via books, pamphlets, public events, debates, and testimony. One of its central focuses is on human life and bioethics.

**The Hastings Center**
21 Malcolm Gordon Rd., Garrison, NY 10524
(845) 424-4040
e-mail: mail@thehastingscenter.org
website: www.thehastingscenter.org

The Hastings Center is an independent research institute that explores the medical, ethical, and social ramifications of biomedical advances. Its website offers videos, books, and the bimonthly *Hastings Center Report* and *IRB: Ethics & Human Research.*

**National Institutes of Health (NIH)**
National Human Genome Research Institute (NHGRI)
9000 Rockville Pike, Bethesda, MD 20892
(301) 402-0911
website: www.nhgri.nih.gov

The NIH is the federal government's primary agency for the support of biomedical research. As a division of NIH, the NHGRI led the Human Genome Project, the federally funded effort to map all human genes, which was completed in 2003. Now the NHGRI has moved into the genomics era with research aimed at improving human health and fighting disease.

**Organic Consumers Association (OCA)**
6771 S. Silver Hill Dr., Finland, MN 55603
(218) 226-4164 • fax: (218) 353-7652
website: www.organicconsumers.org

The OCA promotes food safety, organic farming, and sustainable agricultural practices. It provides information on the hazards of genetically engineered food, irradiated food, food grown with toxic sludge fertilizer, mad cow disease, rBGH in milk, and other issues. Its website offers fact sheets and articles on genetically modified foods.

**US Department of Agriculture (USDA)**
1400 Independence Ave. SW, Washington, DC 20250
website on agricultural biotechnology: www.nal.usda.gov

The USDA is one of three federal agencies, along with the Environmental Protection Agency and the Food and Drug Administration, primarily responsible for regulating US biotechnology. The USDA conducts safety research on genetically engineered organisms, helps form government policy on agricultural biotechnology, and provides information to the public.

**US Food and Drug Administration (FDA)**
10903 New Hampshire Ave., Silver Spring, MD 20993
(888) 463-6332
e-mail: webmail@oc.fda.gov • website: www.fda.gov

The FDA is a public health agency that protects American consumers by enforcing food, drug, and cosmetic health laws. The FDA ensures the safety of the US food supply and enforces labeling of products. It also provides the public with accurate and science-based information through its government documents, reports, fact sheets, and press releases.

## Books

Gessen, Masha. *Blood Matters: From Inherited Illness to Designer Babies, How the World and I Found Ourselves in the Future of the Gene.* New York: Houghton Mifflin Harcourt, 2009. Gessen's straightforward account demonstrates the distance that lies between DNA diagnostics and the discovery of any defective gene. Her personal "journey along the genetic frontier" explores how hard it is to make decisions in the age of genetic engineering.

Glover, Jonathan. *Choosing Children: Genes, Disability, and Design.* New York: Oxford University Press USA, 2008. The author discusses how progress in genetic and reproductive technology offers us the never-before-available option of choosing what kinds of offspring to have. Professor of medical ethics at King's College, London, Glover discusses definitions of disability, which genetic engineering may aim to overcome.

Harris, John. *Enhancing Evolution: The Ethical Case for Making Better People.* Princeton, NJ: Princeton University Press, 2010. Making a clear and ethical case for biotechnology, bioethicist Harris dismantles objections to stem cell research, genetic engineering, designer babies, and cloning. Harris argues that human enhancement is a good thing.

Häyry, Matti. *Rationality and the Genetic Challenge: Making People Better?* Cambridge: Cambridge University Press, 2010. Should we make people healthier, smarter, and longer-lived if medical advances enable us to? Häyry asks this question in the context of genetic testing and selection, stem-cell research, and gene therapies. Ethical questions explored include the use of people as means, parental responsibility, and the dignity of life.

Knowles, Lori P., and Gregory E. Kaebnick. *Reprogenetics: Law, Policy, and Ethical Issues.* Baltimore: Johns Hopkins University Press, 2007. From the cloning of Dolly the sheep to advances in stem-cell research, new genetic technologies can cause ill-informed debate. In this thoughtful collection, Knowles and Kaebnick assemble bioethicists from around the world to examine the ethical challenges created by genetic manipulation.

Robin, Marie-Monique. *The World According to Monsanto: Pollution, Corruption, and Control of Our Food Supply.* New York: New Press, 2010. Winner of the Rachel Carson prize, this book is a disturbing exposé of the practices of the world's most influential multinational agri-corporation.

Smith, Jeffrey M. *Genetic Roulette: The Documented Health Risks of Genetically Engineered Foods,* White River Junction, VT: Chelsea Green, 2007. Discusses sixty-five health risks related to genetically engineered food.

Whitehouse, Beth. *The Match: "Savior Siblings" and One Family's Battle to Heal Their Daughter.* Boston: Beacon, 2011. This book offers a detailed, riveting account of Steve and Stacy Trebing's fight to heal their daughter Katie's rare disease, a condition requiring monthly blood transfusions that would eventually destroy her organs. The Trebings chose to create a "savior sibling," conceived to provide lifesaving bone marrow for Katie.

## Periodical and Internet Sources

Ananda, Rady. "Opening the Door to GM Crops in Europe," Global Research, December 14, 2010. www.globalresearch.ca/index.php?context=va&aid=22404.

Appel, Jacob M. "Mandatory Embryo Genetic Testing Isn't Eugenics, It's Smart Science," *Free Republic* (blog), March 4, 2009. www.freerepublic.com/focus/f-news/2200624/posts.

Beato, Greg. "Billion Dollar Babies: The Brave New World of Designer Babies," *Reason,* March 29, 2009. http://reason.com/archives/2009/03/24/billion-dollar-babies.

Brockman, Terra. "Sustainable Farming, Not Genetically Modified Crops, Will Feed the World," *Zester Daily,* June 16, 2010. www.zesterdaily.com/zester-soapbox-articles/549-fooling-the-world.

Burns, Katie. "Genetically Engineered Animals in the Food Supply," *JAVMA News,* November 1, 2008. www.avma.org/onlnews/javma/nov08/081101a.asp.

Darnovsky, Marcy. "Are We Headed for a Sci-Fi Dystopia?," AlterNet, March 22, 2008. www.alternet.org/movies/80151.

De Greef, Willy. "GM Food for Thought," *European Voice,* November 19, 2009. www.europeanvoice.com/article/imported/gm-food-for -thought/66459.aspx.

Green, Ronald M. "Building Baby from the Genes Up," *Washington Post,* April 13, 2008. www.washingtonpost.com/wp-dyn/content /article/2008/04/11/AR2008041103330.html.

Häyry, Matti. "Savior Siblings," University of Helsinki, Finland, 2010. www.helsinki.fi/collegium/english/staff/Hayry/Publ%20 2010%20liite%204.pdf.

Herper, Matthew. "Green Genes: Are Genetically Modified Crops Eco-Friendly?," *Forbes,* March 1, 2010. www.forbes.com /forbes/2010/0301/opinions-gmos-crops-genetics-monsato-ideas -opinions.htrnl?boxes=businesschannelsections.

Herren, Hans, and Marcia Ishii-Eiteman. "Genetically Modified Crops Are Not the Answer," *Hill,* April 22, 2010. http://thehill .com/opinion/op-ed/93907-genetically-modified-crops-are-not- the-answer.

Hughes, James, interviewed by Brandon Keim. "Designer Babies: A Right to Choose?," Wired.com, March 9, 2009. www.wired.com /wiredscience/2009/03/designerdebate.

Levine, Judith. "What Human Genetic Modification Means for Women," Committee on Women, Population, and the Environment, January 4, 2007. www.cwpe.org/node/170.

McKie, Robin. "Why the Case for GM Salmon Is Still Hard to Stomach," *Guardian* (UK), August 27, 2010. www.guardian.co.uk /environment/cif-green/2010/aug/27/gm-fish-meat-environment.

Mittal, Anuradha. "G8 Summit: Feed the Hungry or Fuel Hunger?," Foreign Policy in Focus, July 8, 2009. www.fpif.org/articles/g8 _summit_feed_the_hungry_or_fuel_hunger.

Moonen, Rick. "Say No to Genetically Engineered Salmon," CNN .com, September 14, 2010. www.cnn.com/2010/OPINION/09/14 /moonen.gmo.salmon/index.html.

National Catholic Bioethics Center. "British Parliament, Human- Animal Hybrids and Savior Siblings," June 3, 2009. www.ncb

center.org/NetCommunity/Page.aspx?pid=482&storyid1277=37&ncs1277=3.

Nelson, Erin, and Timothy Caulfield. "When It Comes to 'Saviour Siblings,' Let's Just Stick to the Facts," *Globe and Mail* (Toronto), July 30, 2009 www.theglobeandmail.com/news/opinions/when-it-comes-to-saviour-siblings-lets-just-stick-to-the-facts/article1195657.

O'Hagan, Andrew. "Some 'Gifts' One Is Better Off Without," *Telegraph* (London), March 11, 2008. www.telegraph.co.uk/comment/columnists/andrewo_hagan/3555996/Some-gifts-one-is-better-off-without.html.

Ozersky, Josh. "How I Learned to Love Farmed Salmon," *Time,* September 1, 2010. www.time.com/time/nation/article/0,8599,2015134,00.html.

Pray, Leslie A. "Embryo Screening and the Ethics of Human Genetic Engineering," *Nature Education,* 2008. www.nature.com/scitable/topicpage/embryo-screening-and-the-ethics-of-60561.

Ropeik, David. "Uh, Oh. FrankenSalmon! Why Is Genetically Modified Food So Scary?," *Psychology Today,* June 28, 2010. www.psychologytoday.com/blog/how-risky-is-it-really/201006/uh-oh-frankensalmon-why-is-genetically-modified-food-so-scary.

Sharratt, Lucy. "Enviropig: A Piggy You Hope Never to Meet at Market," *Common Ground,* June 2010, www.commonground.ca/iss/227/cg227_enviropig.shtml.

Shebaya, Sirine. "Are 'Designer Babies' on the Horizon?," *Science Progress,* May 15, 2008. www.scienceprogress.org/2008/05/designer-babies.

Union of Concerned Scientists. "Failure to Yield: Biotechnology's Broken Promises," Issue Briefing, July 2009. www.ucsusa.org/assets/documents/food_and_agriculture/failure-to-yield-brochure.pdf.

Wilkinson, Stephen. "Couples Should Be Able to Choose Their Baby's Sex," British Broadcasting Company, May 26, 2010. http://news.bbc.co.uk/2/hi/health/8665282.stm.

Zohar, Yonathan. "Genetically Modified Salmon Is Fit for the Table," CNN.com, September 22, 2010. http://articles.cnn.com/2010 -09-22/opinion/zohar.genetically.engineered.salmon_1_fish-and -seafood-wild-stocks-wild-atlantic-salmon?_s=PM:OPINION.

## Websites

**Alliance for Better Foods** (www.betterfoods.org/). The alliance supports biotechnology as a safe way to provide for a more abundant, nutritious, and higher-quality food supply. Articles, news, resources, and regulations with pro–genetically modified organism (GMO) themes.

**The Future of Human Evolution** (www.humansfuture.org/). This site offers a large database of articles and ideas that examine the future of humanity and how science, technology, and evolution may shape our common future. Contains many articles on genetic engineering, disease elimination, human cloning, engineering ethics, life extension, and human improvement.

**Institute for Responsible Technology (IRT)** (www.responsibletech nology.org). The IRT is an online community of scientists and leaders who aim to eradicate genetically modified organisms from the world's food supply. Using grassroots and national strategies, the IRT educates the public about the dangerous health effects of GM foods and fights for public policies that will protect consumers.

# Index

PGE. *See* Preimplantation
genetic diagnosis
Phosphorous
development of pig with lower
production of, 68, 70
environmental effects of, 66,
73
is not sole problem with pig
waste, 74
*See also* Enviropig
Physicians and Scientists for
Responsible Application of
Science and Technology
(PSRAST), 22, 100
Phytase, 68, 73, 76
Pigs, genetically altered,
*67*
Pinker, Steven, 9, 14, 108
Polls. *See* Surveys
Preimplantation genetic
diagnosis (PGD), 33, 94
conditions predicted to be
detected by, 28
in creation of savior siblings,
views on ethics of, *42*
genetic conditions identified
by, 27–28
human embryo in, *27*
process of, *96*
should focus on conditions
with greatest impact on
child's wellbeing, 30
Prenatal testing
impact on births of Down
syndrome children,
7–8
opinion on harm *vs.* benefit
of, *29*

*Principles for the Risk Analysis
of Foods Derived from
Modern Biotechnology* (Codex
Alimentarius Ad Hoc
Intergovernmental Task
Force on Foods Derived from
Modern Biotechnology),
119–120
*Proceedings of the National
Academy of Sciences* (journal),
86
Processed foods, percentage with
GM components, 56
PSRAST (Physicians and
Scientists for Responsible
Application of Science and
Technology), 22, 100

Q
Quintavalle, Josephine, 40

R
Ronald, Pamela, 50
Roundup Ready crops, 61
Royal Association for Deaf
People, 106, 107
Royal National Institute for Deaf
and Hard of Hearing People,
106

S
Salmon, *88*
GE *vs.* standard, growth of, *82*
genetically engineered, could
save fishing industry, 79–80
*See also* AquAdvantage salmon
Sandel, Michael, 16–17
Savior siblings, 38

# Picture Credits